PRAISE FOR
TRUTH PLUS LOVE

With the advent of the internet and, particularly, the prevalence of social media, we all have a platform. Our channels are megaphones through which our opinions, beliefs, and entire lives are shouted to the world. As Jesus followers, we have the responsibility and opportunity to steward these platforms in a way that honors and exalts His name. I can't think of a more qualified voice to lead us in this responsibility than Matt Brown. *Truth Plus Love* will help you follow Scripture's mandate to season your speech—online and in person—with salt (Colossians 4:6). This is a timely read!

Louie Giglio, pastor of Passion City Church,
founder of Passion Conferences

Matt Brown has been a great friend in ministry, and I'm so excited about this powerful book that will help you point others to Jesus with your life. Truth and love are the two callings of the Christian. Without both, we won't be very effective in doing what God has called us to do, but with them both, we can change the world.

Greg Laurie, pastor of Harvest Christian Fellowship,
author, evangelist leading Harvest America

I am thankful for the way Matt Brown entreats us to both truth and love. In today's world there are innumerable opinions, but we have a great need to be reminded of what is truth. The Bible, for thousands of years, has been where many have ascertained truth that has changed their lives and society for the better. We also need more grace—to give other people dignity even when we see issues differently than they do. We need both the truth and love that this indispensable book shares, and we need them now more than ever.

Steve Green, president of Hobby Lobby,
founder of Museum of the Bible

As followers of Jesus, each one of us has been equipped to carry His love and the truth of the gospel into our world. Matt's book will challenge you to live on assignment for Jesus and provide you with practical tools to put that mission into practice.

Christine Caine, bestselling author, founder
of A21 and Propel Women

Our world needs more of the kindness and peace that Matt Brown so beautifully shares about in *Truth Plus Love*. I know you will love this book! There is enough bad news, criticism, and hostility in the world. We need to shine a light on the good all around us. Will you join us in spreading the light? If each of us do our part, we can touch the world.

Roma Downey, actress in *Touched by an Angel*, executive
producer of *The Bible* miniseries, founder of LightWorkers,
and bestselling author of *Box of Butterflies*

Truth Plus Love is a poignant message for today's Christian culture. Using Jesus's example, Matt spurs us onward, reminding us that it is imperative we learn how to meld those two seemingly opposing concepts. It is a must-read as we seek to love others well in the ethos of our ever-fluid world.

Lisa Bevere, *New York Times* bestselling author of *Without Rival*

In this day and age, whether you like it or not, *you* have been handed a megaphone, and with that, your words will reach more people than you ever imagined and carry more weight than you ever expected. In this book, Matt Brown brilliantly exposes and reconciles the seemingly difficult dichotomy of using that megaphone to communicate both truth and love in the same breath. The message and candor in this book could not have come at a more pertinent time in our history. If your goal is to represent Christ to this hurting and broken world, then this book is for you.

Levi Lusko, pastor of Fresh Life Church and bestselling author

What will change the world is not simply talking like a Christians or following popular Christian slogans but returning to the foundational truths and wisdom of the Bible. God calls us to both truth and love. The truths in the Bible have influenced billions of people for thousands of years, more than any other book, and it doesn't show signs of slowing. The Bible also calls us to love others whether we agree with them or not. Truth plus love is our formula to change the world.

Bobby Gruenwald, founder of the YouVersion Bible app

People today need a lot more grace for each other. The kind of grace that flows freely from the kindness of God. God is so loving, kind, and patient with us, and for those of us who follow Him, God calls us to imitate Him to the world. People need to see the grace, love, and kindness of God in our lives and our interactions with them. This can change the world, and that is exactly what my friend Matt Brown calls us to do in this important new book.

Jon Erwin, Erwin Brothers Entertainment, producer of *I Can Only Imagine*, cofounder of Kingdom

In this critical moment in history, Matt Brown issues a clarion call to the church, to return to both life-giving truth and remarkable love. It is both truth and love that should define the entirety of the life of the believer. God has called you to look different from the world around you. You are meant for something more—you are called to be an ambassador of the King of Kings and the Lord of Lords. Now is your moment to step into your high calling in Jesus Christ.

Dr. Samuel Rodriguez, pastor of New Season, president of the National Hispanic Christian Leadership Conference

God's love is the most transformational reality in the universe. It changes hearts and lives. We need to do more than acknowledge it mentally. We need to experience it in deeply our hearts. God's love changes us and sets our lives on a new course. Suddenly, we want to love as many people around us as we can, and our hearts burst to share God's love with the whole world. A new purpose fills our lives—to walk in truth plus love and share it with as many people as we can!

Bobby Schuller, host of *Hour of Power*, pastor of Shepherd's Grove

Not only is Matt Brown a good friend, but he's a good example for all of us of what it means to live with both the truth and love of Jesus. Jesus set the pace, and we are called to follow Him—not only to walk in the truth of the Bible but to overflow with God's grace on a weary and broken world that needs it so much. This book will help you see how to make a real difference in the world!

David A. R. White, actor and producer, cofounder of Pure Flix

There has never been a greater need for Christians to walk in both truth and love. Matt Brown is a great example of this, and I'm grateful he is helping us to see this biblical model and giving us practical tools to walk in both truth and love. When Christians walk in both truth and love, we grow in our influence with our families, in our workplaces, and even throughout the centers of influence across our nation. Now is the time for believers everywhere to begin to speak the truth in love. We need to love one another, and the church must lead the way.

Dr. Ronnie Floyd, senior pastor of Cross Church,
president of the National Day of Prayer

I can't think of a more important message during this pivotal moment in time. Matt skillfully guides us through the lost art of speaking the truth in love. A must-read if you hope to have real influence of those around you.

Ed Eason, guitarist for multiplatinum artists,
including Carrie Underwood

We live in a world of echoes and not voices. Echoes sound like what we have heard before, while voices—true voices—resonate with compelling clarity with something new. My good friend Matt Brown lives his creed in this book. Next-generation leaders are rejecting cheap leadership and long to influence the Jesus way. *Truth Plus Love* is a manual on how to live with significance and lead with biblical vitality. For those who "think eternity" and are worn out with cheap people-manipulation hacks, this book will provoke you to influence and lead in the power and fruit of the Spirit.

Dr. Malachi O'Brien, intercessor, revivalist, and voice

Truth Plus Love is a timely book for the church. We are living in a time when Christians need to understand the importance of speaking and living the truth in love instead of living in hypocrisy and speaking hate. One of my favorite quotes is "A great example preaches a powerful sermon." In my friend Matt Brown's book, you will learn how to preach powerfully by the way you live and in return spread the truth and love that this world so desperately needs.

Remi Adeleke, former Navy SEAL, actor, author of *Transformed*

Truth Plus Love is a powerful book that opens your eyes about what it means to be a person of faith today. Matt gives insight into how the things we use today, such as social media, can be used for good. Matt is a true leader for this generation and many generations to come.

Madeline Carroll, actress, *I Can Only Imagine*

Truth Plus Love is a book for this generation, written at a time when technology gives us immediate access to knowledge about God, but the level of pride we filter that knowledge through has caused the gospel to become a weapon instead of a balm. Matt has issued an inspiring call to all believers to return to the Bible in totality—a faith rooted in the truth of God's Word and a love for God's people. This book has inspired me, convicted me, and reminded me that truth without love can never be the full truth because God is love.

Nona Jones, Nona Jones Ministries, global faith-based partnerships leader at Facebook

Matt Brown is an audacious leader who leans forward into a life of intentional love and genuine influence. He has such a passion to see people come to know Jesus—to have real relationship with Him. This book gives you tangible resources to do the same.

Mack Brock, worship leader, songwriter

I have the great privilege of counting Matt Brown as my friend. To know him is to see *Truth Plus Love* in action. The man is unashamed of the gospel of Christ and shares it boldly. And he is among the kindest, most gracious men I have known. I want to be like him. So when he speaks of *Truth Plus Love*, I listen closely. And I have found much to glean from in this book. Read it with a pen and with prayer. And press to follow more faithfully the Truth (John 14:6) who is also Love (1 John 4:16).

Jon Bloom, cofounder of Desiring God, author of *Not by Sight*

ALSO BY MATT BROWN

Awakening: How God's Next Great Move Inspires
and Influences Our Lives Today

Chosen: What If You Reminded Yourself of the
Gospel Every Day? (with Ryan Skoog)

TRUTH *PLUS* LOVE

THE *JESUS* WAY TO INFLUENCE

MATT BROWN

ZONDERVAN®

*This book is dedicated to the love of my
life, Michelle, with whom I am learning
what it means to love more every day*

ZONDERVAN

Truth Plus Love
Copyright © 2019 by Matt Brown

Requests for information should be addressed to:
Zondervan, *3900 Sparks Dr. SE, Grand Rapids, Michigan 49546*

ISBN 978-0-310-35524-3 (softcover)

ISBN 978-0-310-35526-7 (audio)

ISBN 978-0-310-35525-0 (ebook)

Art direction: Curt Diepenhorst
Interior design: Denise Froehlich

Printed in the United States of America

19 20 21 22 23 /LSC/ 10 9 8 7 6 5 4 3 2 1

CONTENTS

FOREWORD

Years ago I had an opportunity to speak with British pastor John Stott. He asked me about my spiritual journey from atheism to faith, which involved nearly two years of research into the historical evidence for Jesus and his resurrection. I spoke to Stott enthusiastically about my passion to share the facts behind our faith with as many people as I could.

Perhaps Stott sensed that my zeal to convince others about the veracity of Christianity was a bit out of balance. Maybe he feared that my approach was too narrow. Whatever the reason, he offered a comment that forever changed my approach to ministry.

"You know," he said gently, "truth without love is too hard, and love without truth is too soft. We need to look to Jesus for how we can effectively combine them both."

I've carried that caution in my heart ever since—and that's why I'm so glad my friend Matt Brown has written this profound, provocative, and practical book on the need for Christians to exhibit both love and truth in our increasingly skeptical world. Each quality is desperately needed if we are going to share the gospel in the twenty-first century.

I can't think of a better author for this topic. Matt and I have developed a friendship over several years as we have ministered together and shared the message of Christ to groups large and small. I've watched Matt as he has proclaimed the truth about Jesus with a warmth and sincerity that spiritually curious people invariably find winsome and attractive.

While Matt's conviction about the certainty of the Christian message is quickly evident when people encounter him, so is his deep compassion and authentic concern for people who are far from God. I'm thrilled with how God has used his gracious approach to reach so many young people in particular—a generation largely jaded toward Christianity.

In the Sermon on the Mount, Jesus exhorted his followers to be like salt and light—that is, to live the kind of life that makes people thirst for God and which shines his message of hope and grace into dark areas of despair. As much as anyone I've ever known, Matt embodies those metaphors, and by doing so, he has encouraged me to strive to be stronger salt and brighter light in my own life.

In an age when there's so much incivility in our social discourse, Matt offers an antidote for those of us who want to be effective ambassadors for Christ. Today we have a terrific opportunity to contrast our approach with the harsh rhetoric and confrontational demeanor we see so many other people taking, especially on social media.

Inside this book, you'll find encouragement, guidance, biblical wisdom, and practical advice. Matt's personal style shines through. As a result, you'll see why I consider him a model of Christian love and truth.

LEE STROBEL, author, *The Case for Christ* and *The Case for Miracles*

PREFACE

As an evangelist and the founder of Think Eternity, I find that a solid half of our ministry today happens online. So it's hard for me to imagine a time when I owned neither a computer nor a phone! But it's true. I used to brag to my friends in Bible college that I didn't need a cell phone. Even though they were becoming more common at that time, I was determined to curb their influence in my life.

Years later I learned that my ancestors on my dad's side were German Mennonites who immigrated to the United States and found the flat plains of Kansas and southern Minnesota to be much like their former home. Mennonites traditionally regard technology with more suspicion than most people, so maybe my bragging about not having a phone was an unconscious echo of my ancestors' beliefs!

My great-great-uncle Henry Brown was the first Mennonite missionary to China. He and his wife spent their lives there, administering medical care to the sick, preaching the gospel, and establishing churches with indigenous leaders. During the Japanese occupation, he spent time in prison for preaching the gospel. He wrote several books about his work, and while reading them, I was shocked to find that a hundred years before I began traveling and preaching across Minnesota, Henry Brown, as an itinerate preacher, had preached in some of the same places in an effort to raise support for his missionary work. It's possible that we even visited some of the same towns and traveled some of the same roads, sharing the wonderful hope of Jesus Christ!

So perhaps I have deeply rooted reasons for being slow to get on social media. My older brother even forced me onto one of the early platforms by signing me up himself, but as I began to blog, my mind slowly changed. I realized I could use social media on my phone and computer for ministry. In many ways, the digital world is our new missions frontier.

I now spend a lot of my life online, as do most of us. In fact, it's an incredible time to be a Christian because a Wi-Fi connection has given us a larger megaphone than ever before to talk about Jesus. At Think Eternity, we've been doing evangelistic ministry online and through live events for seventeen years.

But we don't always use the internet well, and that's why I've written this book.

On one of our ministry trips to the East Coast years ago, I had a powerful encounter that taught me a lesson about the opportunity and responsibility we have with our online megaphones.

A warm blast of late spring air greeted us as we drove to our host's home in northern Virginia. My wife, Michelle, and I, along with another couple, had been on a preaching tour across the Midwest and down the East Coast for nearly two months. On the last leg of our journey, we anticipated ministering to some great churches on the outskirts of our nation's capital. As we stepped into our hosts' home we were greeted by pictures on the walls of our host with various US presidents and other world leaders. The hallway was lined with thank-you cards and personal greetings from presidents and celebrities.

Our stay had been God-ordained, a needed pit stop after months of travel, and we developed a meaningful, timely friendship with Doug, our host, who is also one of the best writers I know. We spent several weeks with Doug and his wife, and they would make us a big breakfast every morning and shower us with kindness and encouragement. At the time, I'd been working feverishly on my first book, and in the course of our conversations, Doug offered to review my draft. Without my even asking, he wrote one of the kindest endorsements I could've asked for. I felt undeserving to have a *New York Times* bestselling author and former assistant to a US president endorse my writing, but that is just the way he and his wife were: gracious and hospitable in a way that bordered on being magical. Doug's endorsement for my book read in part, "Matt Brown is like a Francis Schaeffer for a new generation."

That was the first I'd ever heard of Schaeffer, so I tracked down a half-century-old book by him called *The Mark of the Christian*, and I sensed God's divine nudge about the importance of truth plus love. Sometimes even a single passage can change your life:

> This attitude [of love toward other Christians and the balance of love and holiness] must be constantly and consciously developed—talked about and written about in and among our groups and among ourselves as individuals.
>
> In fact, this must be talked about and written about *before* differences arise between true Christians. We have conferences about everything else. Who has ever heard of

a conference to consider how true Christians can exhibit in practice a fidelity to the holiness of God and yet simultaneously exhibit in practice a fidelity to the love of God before a watching world? Whoever heard of sermons or writings which carefully present the practice of two principles which at first seem to work against each other: (1) The principle of the practice of the purity of the visible church in regard to doctrine and life, and (2) the principle of the practice of an observable love and oneness among *all* true Christians.

If there is no careful preaching and writing about these things, are we so foolish as to think that there will be anything beautiful in the practice when differences between true Christians must honestly be faced?

Before a watching world, an observable love in the midst of difference will show a difference between Christians' differences and other men's differences. The world may not understand what the Christians are disagreeing about, but they will very quickly understand the difference of our differences from the world's differences if they see us having our differences in an open and observable love on a practical level.[1]

Boom. Wow. Who writes like that anymore? And how we need this message today! The necessity for Christians everywhere to walk in both truth and love has only grown since Schaeffer wrote those words.

You may think that writers look for trendy topics that respond to some felt need, but for me, the theme of truth plus love has weighed so heavily on my heart for so long that I can't *not* write about it. This topic is an important one, a vitally important one, and shockingly few people have written about it. For four years now, God has been putting on my heart this idea about the fragile, life-giving balance of truth and love in the life of a Christian.

Today we face bigger giants than ever. Christians all over the world now have something Francis Schaeffer's generation never had: the internet and social media. Now every Christian who is, by default, a representative of Jesus to the watching world, either for good or bad, has a megaphone through their social media accounts. They can instantly proclaim whatever comes to their mind and whatever half-thought-through response they have to any given subject, political issue, or tragedy, whether or not it's what the Bible says about that subject.

More voices are shouting more loudly and more frequently than ever before, and therefore our need to understand Francis Schaeffer's words about truth and love is greater than ever before.

Important Questions for Christians Today

How should Christians engage with, and respond to, a watching world?

How should Christians represent both the love and the truth of Jesus?

Do we need to respond to every controversy, tragedy, or problem that arises in our world?

Why is our world filled with so many broken relationships?

How can some Christians be so sweet in person but so angry on their social media accounts?

What would happen if more Christians brought their statements in line with both the love and the truth that the Bible talks about?

In this book, I speak about these questions and many more. I hope that, like me, you will see that we, as Christians, have a biblical mandate to walk in both truth and love—a mandate that could change the whole world.

And now, with Francis Schaeffer's half-century-old call echoing in my heart and prompting me onward, let's get started.

CHAPTER 1

WHERE HAS OUR INFLUENCE GONE?

Rather, speaking the truth in love, we are to grow up in every way into him who is the head, into Christ.

EPHESIANS 4:15 ESV

As I sipped the golden brown foam off the top of the most delicious cappuccino I've ever tasted—my wife, Michelle, and I looked out from the crowded coffeehouse, across the cobblestone streets, to the Pantheon, one of the wonders of ancient Rome. Once used for the worship of various gods, the Pantheon eventually became a worship hall for Christians, and now, two thousand years later, it overflows with tourists for it still captivates the imagination with awe and wonder. It is an architectural masterpiece in the heart of Rome, just blocks from the Vatican, and a twenty-minute walk from the Colosseum. So much history has unfolded in these streets. My taste buds—as well as my mind—were exploding with sensory overload and bliss.

I'd long wanted to visit the nation of my Italian grandmother Longiotti's roots. The opportunity finally came after Michelle and I had been married a few years, and we decided to visit Milan, Florence, and Rome. Milan had the feel of a global city, with a lot of high-end shopping. Florence had the air of old Italy. And Rome, once the epicenter of the earth, is the eternal city, home to not only the Vatican but countless ancient wonders. There you find the modernity of today's world, but you can also get lost in the cobblestone streets and artifacts, not to mention the pizza, spaghetti, and coffee of a past world.

Two quaint coffee shops near the Pantheon transported me to coffee heaven: La Casa del Tazza d'Oro and Sant'Eustachio Il Caffè. Let me say that the coffee in pretty much any coffee shop in Italy tastes better than the best coffee in the US, but that being said, the coffee in these two shops tasted like liquid gold. I don't know how it's possible for something to taste that good.

Rome was breathtaking. Aside from getting lost on cobblestone walkways, admiring the architecture, and savoring the food, we visited many ancient sites, including the Colosseum. This is where countless gladiators were forced to do battle in front of thousands of onlookers who jeered and cheered the warriors to their death. It's hard to believe that any culture could be so callous as to make sport out of something like this, but it's part of our human story.

Christians have always been at odds with the culture around them, and the first Christians were no exception. At times, the Roman Empire persecuted Christians for worshiping Jesus rather than the Emperor. Christians claimed to be part of a different kingdom, and for that they were perceived as a threat. Much of this persecution happened right there in the Colosseum. We paid to gain entrance and wound down the ancient stairwells and peered into the underground halls and closures that housed both victims and animals.

It was here that ancient Christians knelt and cried out to God for deliverance before being fed to the beasts in front of the mocking crowds. There are no words to express the horror of what took place. The savagery that Christians have endured throughout history, including being persecuted around the world today, reminds us of the mind-boggling value of our faith. Those Christians could have simply denied Jesus and been set free, but they valued what Christ meant to them more than their own lives.

After our tour, we visited a few other ancient buildings and then wound our way back around the Colosseum in search of lunch. After a quick bite, we continued down the street and stumbled upon an old church. Its underground passages seemed to take us farther and farther back in history until, at the bottom of the site, we entered rooms and halls where some of the very first Christians worshiped and prayed. Most likely, they prayed for some of their own who were being taken to the Colosseum to their deaths. They prayed for their communities and their city and the world that the message of Jesus would be carried far and wide through their witness. They prayed for, and possibly along with, the apostle Paul and the apostle Peter before both of those men were martyred in the city. We were breathing the air of legends!

As we wound down those stairs, deeper and deeper into the roots of our collective Christian faith, we couldn't help but sense the magnitude of what we've inherited today in Christ, in the church. This isn't some newfound faith, where we get to make up the rules as we go. We stand on the shoulders of all those who have gone before us, with their abiding faith and unforgettable impact on the world. Their faith helps us grasp the gravity of our faith today. Jesus, the Hope of the world, has worked in countless lives through the centuries, including our own.

But sometimes it can feel as if we're doing pitifully little compared to those Christians who gave their lives in the Colosseum or those on whose shoulders of prayers and sacrifice the first churches were built. The gospel spread at breakneck speed long before internet was ever invented. Those early Christians knew that the message had transformed their lives, and they showed it in everything from their passion to spread the gospel to the very act of martyrdom—giving their lives rather than denying the gospel of Jesus Christ.

God has a place and a purpose for us today as well. He wants to build His beautiful kingdom on our shoulders too. He is working in and through us to help us follow Him. He created us and saved us for good works, which He has prepared in advance for us to do. We are part of this great adventure of representing God to our world.

Too often Christians focus exclusively on the message of the gospel. As an evangelist, I know the message is vitally important, but the Bible also has a lot to say about our attitudes and character, about how we talk to others, how we treat them, and how we comport ourselves. Those things are just as important as making sure we get all the doctrinal points correct.

The result of this imbalance has played out in our culture over the past decades as we read such headlines as "Young people are leaving the church in droves." It makes sense if you consider how poorly some Christians represent Jesus these days. Anyone with a social media "megaphone" feels they have the authority to tear others down. Just yesterday I saw someone tear down a pastor I deeply respect, a man who has spent his life teaching the Bible and leading thousands to faith in Jesus. This person publicly scolded him, saying he was "an embarrassment to Jesus" and that God "was ashamed of him." What he said couldn't be farther from the truth.

I see personal attacks like this all the time, and from Christians no less. Christians today are known more for what they are against than what they are for, which is sad, considering we are supposed to have good news to offer the world that already has enough bad news. We see it all the time: Christians who constantly correct each other, rebuke each other, even speak angrily to people they've never met. There's even a hashtag on twitter for this: #JesusJuke, which means using the Bible to one-up or correct strangers on the internet who you think are wrong.

Nowhere in Scripture does God give us permission to be a jerk. It's that kind of Christianity that turns people away from the gospel every single day. How is the world supposed to see the grace of God if the people of God are not gracious? We have a problem when we try to do the Great Commission without the compassion of Christ.

Truth Plus Love

Maybe I spend too much time on social media, but I see it every day—Christians who are supposed to be marked by the love of Christ who sound anything but loving. There is too much angry, critical, cynical, judgmental Christianity in the world. Too many Christians are trying to prove their point and to have the last word. But I believe if they could see what the Bible says about this, they would see how God wants them to grow in their faith in ways they've neglected before.

The Bible talks a lot about truth plus love. Paul writes about it in his letter to the Ephesians, the first half of which contains no direct commands other than "remember," meaning that he doesn't tell them to "do" anything *new*. Rather, he calls them back to the gospel—the main event of history itself—encouraging them to be captivated by all God has done for them in Jesus. That first chapter contains the largest run-on sentence in the Bible, and twice in the first half of the letter he breaks out into prayer. He cannot contain his excitement about Jesus and what Jesus does in our lives!

Paul prays that these believers—and all believers at all

times—would be captivated and overwhelmed by the gospel and that God would open their spiritual eyes to all they have in Christ. One of the most amazing parts of all of this is that Paul was writing from prison, and yet in spite of his circumstances, he was full of wonder and joy because of the gospel.

The last half of his letter, in contrast to its opening, contains forty direct commands. In other words, he was saying to believers, here is what you do to follow Him. One of these powerful commands is found in the middle of Ephesians 4: "*Speaking the truth in love*, we are to grow up in every way into him who is the head, into Christ" (Ephesians 4:15 ESV, emphasis added).

Did you see it? *Truth plus love.* That is the formula God has given us for influencing our world and living an effective Christian life. God has called us to a balance of both truth and love, not just emphasizing one or the other. If we do that, we will "grow up in every way" in Jesus Christ.

Jesus set the example. One of His closest friends and followers, John, tells us about this balance in Jesus's life: "The Word became flesh and made his dwelling among us. We have seen his glory, the glory of the one and only Son, who came from the Father, *full of grace and truth*" (John 1:14 NIV, emphasis added). Better than anyone Jesus walked in both truth and love, and He calls those of us who follow Him to do the same.

The apostle Paul spoke elsewhere about these two traits: "We prove ourselves by our purity, our understanding, our patience, our kindness, by the Holy Spirit within us, and *by our sincere love. We faithfully preach the truth. God's power is working in us.* We use the weapons of righteousness" (2 Corinthians 6:6–7 NLT, emphasis added). Right in the middle of his list of important traits, Paul says sincere love and faithful preaching of the truth will prove the impact of our faith and ministry. He adds that God's power works in him to do both. Not only do these verses package truth and love together, but you'd be hard pressed to read much of the Bible without seeing those two as its major themes.

Truth and love are the two legs of the Christian. Without both we don't get far. God's power works in us when we walk in both truth and love, and we will be influential for the sake of the gospel.

Solomon, the wisest person before Jesus, affirms this idea: "Whoever *pursues righteousness and love* finds life, prosperity and honor" (Proverbs 21:21 NIV, emphasis added), and "Do not let *kindness and truth* leave you; Bind them around your neck. Write them on the tablet of your heart" (Proverbs 3:3 NASB, emphasis added). And then the New Living Translation adds, "Then you will find favor with both God and people, and you will earn a good reputation" (Proverbs 3:4 NLT). The essential idea is that truth and love work together in harmony to honor God and, through us, influence others for good. The Bible tells us that when we walk in truth and love we find abundant life, honor, favor from God and other people, and a good reputation. Many of these traits can be summarized in one word: *influence*.

If we look thoughtfully at how the Christian is supposed to walk distinctively in both truth and love, we begin to see how we influence our world for good. What if, when a tragedy strikes or a political controversy arises, Christians everywhere responded on their social media feeds with a uniquely Christian graciousness? What if we weren't the first to attack and didn't act like stray dogs hovering over helpless prey, waiting to move in for the kill? What if we expressed an unusual love, an unusual graciousness, and responded with the mind of Christ, keeping in step with the Spirit? What if we spoke the truth, always in love, and what if those words brought healing and comfort and peace to a world that is parched for peace? What if?

Don't get me wrong. Many Christians do this today, but even more do not. A couple of older men I know are incredibly kind in person, but on their Facebook pages they sound like raging maniacs. They stomp all over everyone else's political opinions, and their posts sound angry, bitter, and demeaning. I don't think that's who they really are; they just don't understand how they come across to a watching world. When I read their posts, my blood pressure rises as I sense the toxic nature of their attitude.

Is this who Jesus wants us to be? Is this what He's called His church to do? The Bible speaks clearly against this type of attitude, and we will delve into many of those verses throughout this book.

God has called His people to be influencers for the sake of the gospel, and He has given us a specific set of attitudes to pick up (and some to lay down) to be effective for His cause, in our relationships, and in our interactions with the rest of the world. Think of Jesus—He attracted large crowds wherever He went for both His miracles and His teaching. He spoke the truth, but He was also marked by a profound love, which drew crowds of people, including his disciples, to Him. He wielded both. Truth and love. And that is exactly what God calls each and every Christian to do.

Truth Minus Love = Noise

If we constantly shout the truth of God but don't walk in the love of God, Scripture says we are "nothing." We will sound like a "clanging cymbal" to the world—an annoying noise. We will be weak and ineffective in our witness, and our relationships will be dysfunctional. In short, we won't walk in the abundant life Jesus promised us.

I know a man who was prone to bitterness about nearly everything in our culture. One time he got so angry at the General Mills company that he drove to their headquarters in the Twin Cities and burned boxes of Cheerios on their front lawn. Did he have the right to protest? Yes. Did such an act honor God or help him walk in the peace and joy that Christ offers to us? Not at all. In fact, within a week, sadly, this man died of a heart attack. James said, "Human anger does not produce the righteousness God desires" (James 1:20 NLT).

God did not intend for us to spend our lives being angry about everyone and everything we don't agree with. Instead, God invites us to walk through our lives with supernatural peace. Jesus tells us, "I am leaving you with a gift—peace of mind and heart. And the peace I give is a gift the world cannot give. So don't be troubled or afraid" (John 14:27 NLT).

Love Minus Truth = Error

If we focus solely on the love of God but ignore the truth of God, we lose the power to save.

We live in a unique time. Major denominations are giving license to sin, and many Christians believe that if they are saved by grace, then they can give license for others to sin. But the Bible clearly warns us against this:

> I say this because some ungodly people have wormed their
> way into your churches, saying that God's marvelous grace
> allows us to live immoral lives. The condemnation of such

people was recorded long ago, for they have denied our only
Master and Lord, Jesus Christ. (Jude 4 NLT)

No matter what sin we're mired in, we are saved by grace alone, through faith alone, in Christ alone, but Jesus also calls us to repent and follow Him—to be a follower, not simply a fan. As imperfect as we are, Jesus wants to save us from sin, and He wants us to grow in holiness.

This is a core gospel issue. The fact that Jesus saves us from our sin—and calls us to walk away from sin and toward Him—is a central part of the gospel message. If we move away from the message of the gospel, we lose the power to save.

I know a group of wonderful Christians that meet for church in a nearby town. Their previous church had a large, historic impact, but the parent denomination decided it was permissible, even for one of its leaders, to live in open sexual sin. The congregation did not agree, except for one lone elder who did. That elder maintained the church building and took control of all the church's assets. The senior pastor, most of the staff, and half the congregation had to leave and start a new church but years later, the joy and freedom of this new, fast-growing congregation are about as contagious and beautiful as I've ever seen. God is moving in their midst as they embrace the whole gospel and experience its power.

Truth Plus Love = Influence

If we walk in the delicate balance of truth plus love, we will be influential for the sake of the gospel. This could be one of the most important messages the church needs today.

Your church and denomination might emphasize truth over love or love over truth, but it is imperative to focus on both. Does your pastor preach more about repentance and holiness or about loving people in the community? That may give you a hint about which of these two areas your church may need to hear more about.

Because we all have megaphones through our social media (and through our personal relationships), it is vital that Christians are taught to be led and controlled by the Holy Spirit, not by the flesh. It is important that we represent Jesus well to a watching world.

The Fruit of the Spirit = Influence

Along with truth and love, Christ wants to work other key traits in us: the "fruit of the Spirit." In Galatians 5:22–23, Paul tells us, "The fruit of the Spirit is love, joy, peace, patience, kindness, goodness, faithfulness, gentleness, self-control; against such things there is no law" (ESV).

Those fruits are not just the flannel-board cutouts we learned about in Sunday school. They are powerful life traits that have the potential to transform every aspect of our lives and make us influential and effective everywhere we go. God doesn't only want to save our soul, He wants to move every area of our life onto the path of godly wisdom. He wants to transform our character and our inner life to be like His Son's.

Think about it, have you ever met a person with a whole lot of love? A whole lot of joy? A whole lot of peace? A whole lot of kindness and gentleness? Who wouldn't want to be around someone who exhibits these traits—these fruits produced by the Holy Spirit in the character of the Christian? Who doesn't want to be friends with a person like that? I've never met an encourager without any friends. These are the kind of traits God wants to produce in us as we follow Him, and these are the exact kind of traits that can help us live effective and purposeful lives in the world, as well as giving us extraordinary influence to tell more people about Christ. The fruit of the Spirit in your own life is what helps you be fruitful in the world.

I firmly believe that if we grow in the fruit of the Spirit— love, joy, peace, patience, kindness, goodness, faithfulness, gentleness, self-control—we will be more influential in our homes, our workplaces, our communities, and our world, for the sake of the gospel.

Emotional Intelligence

Over the past few decades, studies have been done and books have been written about what is called Emotional Intelligence. Essentially, researchers studied graduates of Ivy League schools, all of whom had high IQs, but it was their *emotional* intelligence—their EQ—that proved to be the secret of their success.[1] Emotional Intelligence involves how we relate to others and our ability to process the circumstances in life and maintain a healthy perspective, our ability to overcome hardships, and more.

Ironically, this sounds a lot like the fruit of the Spirit. Not to compare apples to apples (no pun intended), but the business world is finally discovering what those who have read the Bible have known for two thousand years!

Things Love to Grow

A few years ago, my cousin Ben and his wife, Sarah, decided to pursue their dream by establishing an internship with an organic farmer in hopes of starting their own farm someday. Eventually they offered crop shares to small groups of people across the Twin Cities. Michelle and I were delighted to sign up.

Every two weeks when they dropped off our fresh vegetables, they would give us a small newsletter describing the contents of each box, along with suggested recipes. In some of them, they included an update from their farm. My favorite story was one that their farm-mentor taught them as they were training to run their own farm. In their first year, they often found themselves nervous about whether they would have enough vegetables for the hundred plus families that had signed up for the crop share. When they got a late start on the season and felt the pressure of being behind in their planting, they would remind themselves of what their farmer-mentor had taught them: "Things love to grow." And sure enough, when the next crop share would roll around, there were always enough vegetables—even more than enough—because green things love to grow.

This is a picture for our lives. When we are connected to Christ, connected to His Word, connected to the local church, the fruit of the Spirit will grow naturally in our lives. Yes, we can work to cultivate them. Yes, we should pursue them. But in His powerful and mysterious way, when we connect to and trust Christ, God will grow the fruit of the Spirit in our lives ... because "things love to grow."

So, while we've lost much of the influence God has intended for His people, the good news is that we know the way back—through truth plus love. Along the way we also need to grow in the fruit of the Spirit, of which love is the beginning and the cornerstone.

But First, Answering Objections

Before we dive into what truth plus love looks like in the real world, let me answer a few of the most common objections—excuses, really—that people raise:

Excuse 1: We don't need to be gracious when we present the gospel. All we need is to tell the truth.

The Bible makes it clear that God calls His people to reflect His character, and that love, humility and gentleness do matter. It tells us to share the truth of God's Word "with gentleness and respect" (1 Peter 3:15) and to "do everything in love" (1 Corinthians 16:14). The Bible says that without love, we will simply be a clanging cymbal (or annoying noise) rendering our Christian lives ineffective.

Excuse 2: Telling people the truth is a loving thing to do. When we speak the truth, we are automatically being loving.

The Bible speaks about truth and love as two distinct, separate traits and tells us we need to walk in both. Yes, we can have others' best interests in mind when we tell them the truth and warn them from harm, but we are still called to do it in a way that is clearly loving and helps them sense that we have their best interests in mind. By contrast, it is completely possible to tell people the truth and turn them away from God by our lack of love.

Excuse 3: *What about being prophetic? What about the Old Testament prophets? And what about Jesus overturning tables in the temple?*

Some people look at the edginess of the Old Testament prophets and use that as an excuse to speak truth harshly. But we are called to follow and imitate Jesus (see Matthew 4:19; Ephesians 5:1), not the Old Testament prophets.

Jesus did overturn tables once, but we know He was without sin, so His anger was righteous. Even righteous anger was a rarity for Jesus. The overarching tone of His life was both profound love and biblical truth. People were drawn to Jesus everywhere He went, because He exuded love and taught truth. There may be times when we feel righteous anger, but we need to be careful to walk in both truth and love.

Some of you might lean toward being more prophetic and intense. If this is the case, you may need to work especially hard at what the Bible clearly calls us to do—to walk in both truth and love.

Excuse 4: *We're not supposed to "try" to be loving. Love is a fruit of the Spirit, a gift from God, not something we can work at possessing.*

The Bible does say that love, joy, peace, kindness, and gentleness are fruits of the Spirit—God's working in us by His Spirit. But the Bible also plainly tells us over and over to pursue these things. Consider that evangelism is a work of the Spirit, but the Bible still calls us to share the gospel. True holiness is Christ saving us and working in us to follow Him, but the Bible still calls us to pursue holiness. We have a part, and God has a part.[2]

Excuse 5: Christians need to stand together and speak the truth loudly to our culture.

It's good for Christians to come together in unity and proclaim the gospel of God's saving grace for struggling sinners. But we must remember 1 Corinthians 13—if we just speak loudly but don't walk in love, we are only a "clanging cymbal" or an annoying noise to our culture. We need both truth and love. We need to love loudly as well.

Excuse 6: The gospel is about grace, so it's not our business to speak truth or tell people not to sin.

The call to turn away from our sinfulness is a core part of the gospel message in several ways: our sin made it necessary for Jesus to give his life on the cross, in order to bridge our separation from God and bring us back into communion with God. Also, the Bible is clear that when we put our faith in Christ, God calls us to repent and turn from our sin. No Christian will ever be perfect in this life, but as we learn to follow Jesus, spiritual growth should occur. Even though we will never be perfect, the Bible warns strongly against giving "license to sin" (or telling people they are okay to live in sinful habits). Jesus came to save us from our sin, not make us feel comfortable with it.

We are saved by grace alone, through faith alone, in Christ alone, but the Bible is clear that true faith results in a lifelong desire to follow Christ and walk away from sin. Because we've experienced nearness to God, we found something better than living in the pigsty of sin. There is a difference between stumbling as we follow Jesus and living comfortably in sinful ways. The core of the gospel message includes the themes of both love and grace, repentance and truth.

Excuse 7: I'm not naturally loving, peaceful, kind, or gentle, so why should I change?

The call of Jesus is a call to "die daily"—to lay down our lives, pick up our cross, and "put on" Christ. We are called to allow Jesus to live his life in and through us. It's not that he wants to change our personality so much as it's that he wants to build in us true character.

Romans 12:6–8 tells us,

> In his grace, God has given us different gifts for doing certain things well. So if God has given you the ability to prophesy, speak out with as much faith as God has given you. If your gift is serving others, serve them well. If you are a teacher, teach well. If your gift is to encourage others, be encouraging. If it is giving, give generously. If God has given you leadership ability, take the responsibility seriously. And if you have a gift for showing kindness to others, do it gladly. (NLT)

And if you don't know how God has gifted you, ask the other believers in your life.

God has gifted us all in different ways. He has given us different levels of faith and different graces to serve His kingdom. Our life circumstances, how we were raised, and the experiences we've gone through may shape or hinder our natural bent toward being loving, joyful, or peaceful. But that doesn't mean we are off the hook. The Bible makes it clear that the fruit of the Spirit is God's consistent goal for every Christian. We won't all have the same level of ease at being loving, joyful, peaceful, or kind, but we are still called by God to work toward them.

The Pressure Makes the Diamond

They say the pressure makes the diamond. And the more pressure, the better. Scripture tells us God's power is perfected in our weakness (2 Corinthians 12:9). I've experienced more than my fair share of pressure, and I've been a witness to too much harshness, vitriol, hate, and just plain evil from other people, including some self-professing Christians. I've experienced hundreds of harsh criticisms over the past seventeen years of doing ministry. Most of this has been from people who didn't know me well. I've had people attack my motives, say horrible things about me, and correct my theology harshly, without love or compassion.

I've experienced hurt, spiritual abuse, and disappointment from church leaders and mentors who focused too much on legalism and lacked an understanding of how to balance it with kindness, gentleness, and love. These leaders invested in my life spiritually but ultimately seemed more interested in building followers who were dependent on them, not raising up others to be leaders. One mentor, for example, after I served for years in his ministry, told me he could never see me as a friend, only as someone he once mentored. He always cloaked these kinds of hurtful statements in spiritual talk, saying all the right things, but ultimately leaving a trail of confused, abused, and hurt interns wherever he went. It's all too easy for us to cloak hurtful words in spiritual talk.

When I was younger and growing in my faith, some of the most passionate Christians I knew were also some of the most unloving and unkind. Don't get me wrong, I knew many loving Christians back then, but I noticed that the people who acted the most passionate were often missing kindness and love. Take for instance a youth leader I knew: he was passionate about memorizing Scripture and sharing his faith, but he was abrasive, legalistic, and sometimes downright mean toward students he didn't think were spiritual enough. Actually, scratch that, *no one* was spiritual enough to satisfy him. But I don't blame him only. There seemed to be an unspoken belief in our churches that God is looking for intense Christians, but really, He is looking for those who exhibit both truth and love.

There have been times when I have been too intense as well. As a young preacher, I sometimes held people to an unrealistic spiritual standard, coming across as aggressive and high-and-mighty. This is why I am now so passionate about this message of truth plus love. When I was younger, I was aiming at the wrong things, and now I find myself longing for God to produce true spiritual maturity in my life. I long to walk in the fruit of the Spirit toward my family, my friends, and those I cross paths with in my life. I long to find the balance between truth and love.

I have learned that over-intensity is false spiritual maturity. God's Word says, "The wisdom that comes from heaven is first of all pure; then peace-loving, considerate, submissive, full of mercy and good fruit, impartial and sincere" (James 3:17). I have learned that no matter how passionate some Christians seem, or how spiritual they talk, there are subtle signposts that show whether true spiritual maturity is present … things like whether they keep their word, if they own up to their mistakes and apologize, if they are focused on serving others, rather than desiring others to serve them, and if they are even-tempered, gentle, peaceful, considerate, full of mercy, and exhibit other fruits of the Spirit. You can't fake those things for long. No one is perfect, but the Bible distinguishes between spiritual immaturity and spiritual maturity and teaches that we can take steps, with His strength and help, down the path toward maturity.

We have to be careful not to be fatalists. Even though we will always fall short and always need the gospel—it is wrong to assume we can never get better at following Jesus. The reason people assume things will never change is that spiritual growth is often painfully slow. But even though we are not yet who we want to be, we can thank God that we are nowhere near who we used to be! He is making all things new.

James reminds us, "We all stumble in many ways" (James 3:2). Any Christian who denies having faults, imperfections, and struggles is contradicting the Word of God. I am far from perfect in these areas myself. But I can tell you as someone who was raised in the church, I simply did not understand the glory, beauty, and magnitude of these traits until recently. God has been opening my eyes. Here is where my heart is: I long to grow in these areas. I'm hungry for God to help me exhibit these fruit in my life!

My life experiences have led me up to this moment—to writing this book. It is my prayer that the burdens I've carried, the tears I've shed, the painful lessons I've learned, and the comfort and wisdom I've received from God's Word as I've walked through these painful trials will serve to flood your own heart with comfort, wisdom, and power from God.

CHAPTER 2

LOVE

God's love has been poured out into our hearts through the Holy Spirit, who has been given to us. . . . God demonstrates his own love for us in this: While we were still sinners, Christ died for us.

ROMANS 5:5, 8

It's been said that our relationship with our earthly father affects how we see our heavenly father. Whether we like it or not, our relationship with our parents will help or hinder us from understanding God's love for us.

Maybe your father was absent or neglectful or not a part of your life. Maybe he was abusive or hurtful. Maybe he was too busy to play with you, spend quality time with you, or go to your games. Maybe he worked hard to support your family, but though you knew he loved you, you wished he could have shown it better. Our experiences as children affect our view of God and His love for us more than we realize.

I've always known my dad loves me, but there were moments when he lost his temper, especially with my mom and occasionally with me and my three brothers. He was never physically abusive, but he struggled with anger. While he did so many things right, I'd be lying if I said that his yelling didn't affect me. I still carry the hurt with me every day, the fragility and brokenness I witnessed, even as a Christian. My dad was a hard worker. I can imagine the pressure he felt to support his family and raise four boys. I'm not saying we didn't ever deserve discipline, but there were times when his anger got out of control. Thankfully, whenever he blew up at us, an hour or so later he would call us to him, hug us, and apologize when needed. Those apologies meant more than he knows.

Once his sons were grown and out of the house, my dad's

mood improved. Now he gets to enjoy life more, play soccer with his grandkids, and be the doting grandfather. He spoils my mom, compliments her often, and loves her well.

I remember one time, when I was a little older, when he'd been especially nasty to my mom. I mustered the courage to bring my Bible to him and share a verse about how husbands are supposed to treat their wives. Like a dog with its tail between its legs, he humbly accepted my correction. But more often than not, his anger went on unchecked.

My mom was used to this treatment. As a surprise child of her parents, nearly fifteen years younger than her older sister, she grew up hearing she'd been unwanted. She suppressed the memories of her mom's nastiness in her childhood, but every so often I've been able to pull the stories out of her, and they are appalling.

When my mom fell in love with and married my dad, she was in marital bliss—for a year or so. But as they began to fight, she quickly realized that even the love she felt for Dad couldn't fill the hole in her heart. My dad had given his life to Christ at a Methodist church in Western Florida in his teens. He was a military kid. My grandparents moved from base to base throughout his growing-up years. He dutifully told my mom about Christ after they were married, in her moments of despair. She had grown up in church but had no real faith of her own, and her parents didn't seem to have any real faith either, just empty religion. At that moment, in their early years of marriage, she too trusted in Christ, and it changed everything in her life. She internalized the words of Augustine, "Our hearts are restless, until they rest in God."

People who meet my mom would be shocked to know

what she has gone through because she embodies such joy, love, peace, kindness, gentleness, and goodness. She embodies truth plus love. She would be the first to say it is Christ's work inside of her. She is not perfect either, but she is a model of the kind of gracious living that is possible through Christ's work in a person's life. No matter who you are, no matter what you have gone through, no matter how well your parents loved you . . .

Christ can change your heart.
Christ can be your peace.
Christ can fill your heart with the love you crave.
Christ can change you from the inside out.
Christ can be all you've ever needed.

Through Christ, you can be the change that your family needs.

Jesus truly changes everything, and often it is in all the little ways we respond to others, our attitudes about life, and the way we treat those closest to us.

It pains me to write all this about my dad because he is a best friend, hero, and role model. No one can take the place of a dad in a kid's life. I still find myself, as an adult, craving his attention, affirmation, and love. Maybe there are other young dads out there like him who love the Lord but are making some of the same mistakes he did. Or young moms who are struggling in their marriage and struggling to see their value and worth. Or sons or daughters who are questioning the love of God because their world is full of pain and brokenness.

My dad has always loved the Bible, and many mornings I would catch him reading it. He served as an elder at our church for many years and has always served our local church faithfully every time the doors are open. He loves the church. He loves his family. He has a strong faith. But as with all of us, that doesn't always mean he was always good at walking in the grace, patience, and self-control that God intends for us to have.

Our churches are filled with well-meaning Christians who know God's truth but don't walk in love, joy, peace, patience, kindness, goodness, or self-control. But the thing is, these fruits actually make us influential for the truth in our families, our workplaces, our communities. Often, the power to walk in the fruit of the Spirit to which the Bible calls us seems just out of reach, beyond our power to grasp and maintain. Life gets busy, things happen, and anxieties rise in our soul:

Am I enough?
Do I have what it takes?
Will this job be stable and help me provide for my family?
What do I need to worry about around the corner?
Why don't I ever have enough me-time?
Why do I feel so exhausted?
Why can't I control my anger?

I know because I've been there. More often than I want to admit. I can identify with the book title by Lane Adams so many years ago, *Why Am I Taking So Long to Get Better?* Lane wrote about his struggle with anger toward his family, even while he served as a pastor. As an associate evangelist for Billy Graham's ministry for many years, he had access to godly teaching, and yet the struggle to walk in patience and self-control stubbornly remained in his life. There have been moments with my own kids when I have acted out angrily. None of us are exempt. All of us need to learn to allow God to work in us to make us people who are more loving and more patient—especially with the people who matter most to us.

What has your relationship with your parents shown you about God? Or how has that relationship hindered and kept you from understanding the love of God? You may have to wade through some memories you'd rather push aside. You may have to confront some of those memories, because moving forward in the Lord requires dealing with the past and understanding where our emotions, and ultimately our split-second attitudes and actions, are stemming from.

So come with me on the journey, and see how God is not afraid to walk with you there, and how even in our great imperfections, He calls us forward to a new way of thinking and living that can change the trajectory of generations who come after us.

The Love the World Needs to See

The kind of love that can change the world is an expressly Christian kind of love. It is a love for others that can only be fueled and motivated by the cross, shed blood, and resurrection of Jesus Christ.

We know what love is because God first loved us.[1] Love was God's idea in the first place.[2] How else would we know what love looks like without seeing all that Jesus gave for us on the cross? God proved His love once for all. Countless people may say the words "I love you" and mean it in countless different ways, but when God says, "I love you," He means it like no one ever has. He loves you so much He left the glory of heaven,

TRUTH PLUS LOVE

became man, and gave His life for you on a cross. On the third day He rose again and soon ascended to sit at the right hand of the Father, as the Name above all names, to spend all of eternity loving all those who would accept His love. But He's a gentleman. He doesn't force His love on anyone.

God not only calls Christians to "do everything in love" (1 Corinthians 16:14), but He first shows us how to "do everything in love" by sending His Son to walk the earth and reveal in countless deeds and words, and ultimately His death and resurrection, the love of the Father. A child who has had a parent who is loving and wise will grow up to love their own children better. This is infinitely truer in our experience of God's love. When we know how loved we are by our Father in heaven, it changes how we are able to love those around us.

My grandmother-in-law used to tell my wife that we all have a "love bank." When someone loves us well, it deposits coins in our love bank. If someone picks on us at school and our love bank is full, it won't affect us. As we grow older, if we are tempted to look for love in the wrong places, yet our love bank is full, we won't have such a difficult time doing the right thing. This is what happens when you see how Jesus loves you ... suddenly your "love bank" is filled up, and you have more love to give to others.

The kind of deep love God calls us to give to our families, friends, fellow Christians, neighbors, communities, and even our enemies is such that it can only be fueled by God's love inside of us. We don't have enough love in ourselves to keep up, but when our hearts believe in God's love through Jesus, and when "God's love has been poured out into our hearts through the Holy Spirit, who has been given to us" (Romans 5:5), we suddenly begin to overflow to the people around us. We love others best when we experience God's love. That is what we need more of: connection to God and His love, for our hearts and our spiritual eyes to be opened to how much He loves us, whereby we can become a conduit of His love into our world.

It can be difficult to grasp God's incomprehensible love for us. We've heard it a thousand times, but it skips past our comprehension, sounding like make-believe. We hear it, we repeat it, but we struggle to believe it. It hasn't penetrated our heart and soul. When it does, it changes us. Our heart softens when we come to understand God's love. It is a beautiful thing to experience.

Grasping the love of God means journeying the eighteen-inch gap between head knowledge and heart knowledge, and that is something that many of us never do. We know what the Bible says, but we can't understand why God would love us so much. When we finally grasp His love, deep down, it changes us and changes how we love the people around us.

Paul wrote about this in Ephesians, praying that our spiritual eyes would be opened to how much God loves us and how much He has done for us in Christ. He showed us how important it is to pray for this in our own lives. If you want to see more of this, you can simply ask God to open your eyes. We need God to help us see the magnitude of His love for us. Paul also talked about the benefits of Jesus in the first few chapters of Ephesians. There is something about mulling over all the good things you have because of Jesus . . . all the ways He has loved you and changed you . . . reading about them in God's Word and meditating on them can help you understand more of the magnitude of God's love for you as well.

It Was Like News from a Far Country

I've long been fascinated by D. L. Moody, the popular American evangelist of the nineteenth century. He grew up poor in rural New England, and his father died tragically while Moody was still young, leaving his mother and seven siblings to fend for themselves. There were times when they could barely rub two cents together, without enough firewood to keep them warm during the harsh New England winters. Thankfully, Moody's mother had older brothers who looked out for the family in their most dire moments.

At seventeen, Moody moved to Boston to make a life for himself, finding work in his uncle's shoe store. He was rough around the edges and utterly uneducated, but as part of his employment, he was required to attend local Sunday school classes to help stave off bad influences in his life. After some months, his Sunday school teacher, a man named Edward Kimball, felt a God-given burden to talk with each of his students individually about their faith in Jesus. One day Kimball visited Moody while he was in the back of his uncle's store stocking shoes, and he confronted him about whether or not he had truly put his faith in Christ. Moody was moved and at that moment responded to the gospel.

Moody quickly grew passionate about his newfound faith. Even his move to Chicago to look for work didn't hamper his enthusiasm for what Christ had begun to mean to him. Long before becoming a powerful preacher, he was an "inviter." The love of Christ had changed him. Not subtly. Dramatically. Everything had changed. He had grown up without the love of a father, and the world had been hard on him. He had to earn his way. Poverty and hardship had already taken their toll, but in the message of the cross, he learned he had been loved all along, by the God who names the stars. And this God had given everything for him in sending Jesus to pay the penalty for his sins.

Moody was moved, and now he wanted to help other young delinquents in the inner city of Chicago, his new home. Moody would gather hundreds of students not only into his own Sunday school class but into all the other Sunday school teachers' classes. He would go into the roughest areas of the city and convince street kids that they should join him for church. He was like a magnet. Classes were rowdy to say the least, but he slowly made an indelible impact on many of those students, an impact that is still felt today. Moody went on to preach the gospel to countless people around the world. After his death, three United States presidents spoke about his impact on them.

One of my favorite stories about Moody is told by his son-in-law. Moody was preaching in Ireland and was approached by a young man named Henry Moorhouse, who had earned the nickname "the boy preacher" because he was beardless and looked young for his age. Moorhouse begged Moody for the opportunity to visit him in the United States and to preach at Moody's church in Chicago. Moody tried to ward him off and thought he'd succeeded until a few weeks after he returned home, he got a letter from Moorhouse stating he was now in America and would like to come preach for Moody if Moody wanted. Moody did not think this "boy preacher" could actually preach, so he wrote him a cold letter, trying to hint in every possible way that he wasn't interested, but if Moorhouse happened to come his way, to come by for a visit. Moorhouse's next letter stated that he would be in Chicago the following Thursday.

Moody told the leaders of his church that Moorhouse was coming and that, while Moody was out of town for a few days, they had probably better let him preach. When Moody returned, he asked his wife how the Irishman preacher had done. She told him it had gone well and that both sermons had been from the text John 3:16: "God so loved the world, that he gave his only begotten Son, that whosoever believeth in him should not perish, but have everlasting life" (KJV). Moody attended the next five nights and later described the experience:

> He preached the most extraordinary sermons from that verse. He did not divide the text into secondly and thirdly and fourthly—he just took it as a whole, and then went through the Bible, from Genesis to Revelation, to prove that in all ages God loved the world.
>
> I never knew up to that time that God loved us so much. This heart of mine began to thaw out, and I could not keep back the tears. It was like news from a far country. I just drank it in.
>
> He could turn to almost any part of the Bible, and prove it. He just beat it down into our hearts, and I have never doubted it since.
>
> I used to preach that God was behind the sinner with a double-edged sword, ready to hew him down. I have got done with that. I preach now that God is behind the sinner with love, and he is running away from the God of love.
>
> On the final night, Moorhouse came to the pulpit and said: "My friends for a whole week I have been trying to tell you how much God loves you, but I cannot do it with this poor stammering tongue. If I could borrow Jacob's ladder,

and climb up into heaven, and ask Gabriel, who stands in the presence of the Almighty, if he could tell me how much love the Father has for the world, all he could say would be: 'God so loved the world, that he gave his only begotten Son, that whosoever believeth in him should not perish, but have everlasting life.'"[3]

This is a powerful testimony from a leader whom many know and admire. Even Moody, with all his passion for the Lord, needed to be awakened to the vastness of God's love! After many years of ministry, he still had more to learn about the love of God. One of Moody's biographers highlights how influential Moorhouse became in his life and ministry. You never know who might teach you about the beauty of God's love, but you should thank them when they do.

God Loves You More in a Moment Than Anyone Could in a Lifetime

Do you recognize this good news? God loves you more in a moment than anyone could in a lifetime. God knows the worst about you, yet He's the one who loves you the most. God has given us His Son, His Holy Spirit, and His Word—all in an effort to express His great love for us. This is the message and hope of the gospel. God loves you, and His love is not faulty and inconsistent like man's love. In fact, God's love is exactly what you were born for: to know it, to receive it, to experience it, to be saturated in it. The satisfaction, the peace, the joy, the purpose and yes, the love you are looking for can only be found in Jesus's great love for you. Only when you believe and receive

His love will your soul truly be satisfied. Nothing else fulfills. Read what the Bible says about the love of God for you, and like Moody, maybe this will be "like news from a far country." Just drink it in. Never doubt it from this point on. Take a moment and pray that God will open your heart to not only hear the words but realize God's love in a way you never have. Try putting your own name into these verses:

For God so loved [say your name here] that he gave his only Son, that whoever believes in him shall not perish but have eternal life. (John 3:16)

But God shows his love for [your name here] in that while we were still sinners, Christ died for us. (Romans 5:8 ESV)

For great is his steadfast love toward [your name here]. (Psalm 117:2 ESV)

The LORD appeared to us in the past, saying: "I have loved [your name here] with an everlasting love; I have drawn you with unfailing kindness. (Jeremiah 31:3)

His banner over [your name here] is love. (Song of Songs 2:4)

The LORD your God is in your midst, a mighty one who will save; he will rejoice over you with gladness; he will quiet you by his love; he will exult over [your name here] with loud singing. (Zephaniah 3:17 ESV)

For the mountains may depart and the hills be removed, but my steadfast love shall not depart from [your name here], and my covenant of peace shall not be removed," says the Lord, who has compassion on you. (Isaiah 54:10 ESV)

See what great love the Father has lavished on [your

name here], that we should be called children of God! And that is what we are! (1 John 3:1 NLT)

Who shall separate [your name here] from the love of Christ? Shall tribulation, or distress, or persecution, or famine, or nakedness, or danger, or sword? As it is written, "For your sake we are being killed all the day long; we are regarded as sheep to be slaughtered." No, in all these things we are more than conquerors through him who loved us. For I am sure that neither death nor life, nor angels nor rulers, nor things present nor things to come, nor powers, nor height nor depth, nor anything else in all creation, will be able to separate us from the love of God in Christ Jesus our Lord. (Romans 8:35–39 ESV)

Love Is the Greatest Thing God Has Told Us to Do

God loves us and calls us to love others well. Paul wrote to the Ephesians, "Live a life filled with love, following the example of Christ. He loved us and offered himself as a sacrifice for us, a pleasing aroma to God" (Ephesians 5:2 NLT). Jesus was asked by a man what the greatest commandment in the law was. Since there are 631 commandments in the Old Testament, Jesus took the opportunity to sum them up: "He answered, 'Love the Lord your God with all your heart and with all your soul and with all your strength and with all your mind'; and, 'Love your neighbor as yourself'" (Luke 10:27).

Every Christian has a high calling to love God and love others. Love is the greatest thing God has told us to do. 1 Corinthians 16:14 tells us to "do everything in love." To the best of our ability, and, even more so, to the best of God's ability through us. We need to realign our lives to focus more on loving others well.

Our love is a language the world can understand. People often don't care how much we know until they know how much we care. Yes, the gospel needs to be proclaimed boldly and clearly, but that alone is not enough. Our lives need to boldly and clearly reveal the love of God to a world starving for true love.

There are many definitions of love in our world today, but 1 Corinthians 13 gives the clearest parameters for what love really looks like. Paul writes:

> If I speak in the tongues of men or of angels, but do not have love, I am only a resounding gong or a clanging cymbal. If I have the gift of prophecy and can fathom all mysteries and all knowledge, and if I have a faith that can move mountains, but do not have love, I am nothing. If I give all I possess to the poor and give over my body to hardship that I may boast, but do not have love, I gain nothing.
>
> Love is patient, love is kind. It does not envy, it does not boast, it is not proud. It does not dishonor others, it is not self-seeking, it is not easily angered, it keeps no record of wrongs. Love does not delight in evil but rejoices with the truth. It always protects, always trusts, always hopes, always perseveres. (1 Corinthians 13:1–8, 13)

Too often this passage is only applied to marriage, which is a shame, because loving God and others is so important. This passage is for all of us, to show how we should love everyone. Think of your family. Think of your friends. Think of your coworkers, or maybe even your boss. Think of your church, small group, and fellow believers. Think of people who are different than you. Think, even, of people who are difficult to love.

We may have great spiritual gifts, great wisdom or intellect, lots of degrees, great faith, great ministry to the poor, but all of this can still be done without a heart of love. If we miss out on truly having a heart of love, we have nothing!

Maybe you feel like you've been doing your best, speaking up for what's right, trying to make God's wisdom clearer. But if our lives are lacking in love, we will be ineffective. Influence and impact come from a person who truly loves other people.

"Love is patient. Love is kind." The fruit of the Spirit describe what it means to live out the others. The fruit of the Spirit complement, harmonize, and build on each other.

"Love doesn't envy, boast, or dishonor others. It isn't proud. It is not easily angered. It doesn't keep a list of failures." Do you come across as boastful when you post on Instagram? When you comment on other people's posts, do you celebrate them or sarcastically tease them?

"Love isn't self-seeking." We don't love others so we can get something out of them. We love people who can do nothing for us.

"Love does not delight in evil but rejoices with the truth." True love is pure and honoring to God and His Word.

"Love protects, trusts, hopes, perseveres." Real love is a steady, consistent, God-given ability to keep on doing what's in another's best interest.

In this broken world, it can sometimes seem like the kind of love described here is far from present reality, but rest assured that God is pouring this kind of love into believers' hearts every day by His Spirit—leaving a beautiful ripple effect in our world.

Do Small Things with Great Love

One of the most incredible examples of living a life of selfless love is Mother Teresa. Michelle and I had the privilege of visiting Calcutta and seeing her ministry there. We were invited by one of her friends, Huldah Buntain, who had also spent her life ministering to the lost and forgotten in Calcutta. Huldah was actually the one who took care of Mother Teresa in her dying days, after Mother Teresa had spent her life doing exactly that for so many others. Mother Teresa spent her life collecting dying children out of the slums and garbage heaps of that city built on a literal swamp during British rule. She would gather the children, care for them, and if there was no hope left, she would give them dignity in death. This is what godly love looks like: Caring for those the world has thrown to the curb. Doing things for people who can never help you back. Spending your life serving those in greatest need. Mother Teresa said, "We can do no great things. We can only do small things with great love." What does this look like in your life—your everyday, sometimes-mundane, sometimes-exhausting daily schedule of work, family, friends, and leisure? Do you see how your caring, your listening, your loving can be, in the words of Mother Teresa, "small" but with "great love"? That is where the adventure of loving people the way God loves you begins.

When your heart has been transformed by God's love, just saying you love people is not enough. You are compelled to show your love by the way you act, by your responses and your good works. 1 John 3:18 says, "Little children, let us not love in word or talk but in deed and in truth" (ESV). We need to consider how our life lines up with these challenges:

- Do you tell your spouse, your children, and your friends how much they mean to you, but you struggle to give them your time, energy, or attention because you are too distracted by work or checking your phone?
- Maybe you tell your family you love them, but the pressures of work, finances, calendar items, or even your drive for perfection cause you to boil over with anger at times, counteracting and working against the loving words you speak to them?
- Do you find your heart locked up from past unforgiveness, pain, or shame that you haven't dealt with, that keeps you from deep emotional connection with your spouse or your children?

We will never be perfect. We will fail in big ways. But God teaches us in His Word how to get back up, not lose heart, and to slowly, surely change for the better. God is always working to teach us how much He loves us and how to love as He loves.

So start with this: tell your family you love them, are proud of them, and how much they mean to you. We all need to do this more, but think of ways you can also line up your actions with your words, and show them how much they mean to you in practical ways. For instance, show up from work on time to spend time with them. Take a few minutes at the end of the work day to be present with them in the time you have together. Surprise your spouse in little ways that delight them, reminding them you love them and think about ways to please them.

In all these situations and more, God wants to teach us by His Word, in practical, down-to-earth ways, how to walk in love. He wants to constantly refill our hearts with His love and teach us how to walk in love toward those closest to us by how we order our daily schedules, by our habits, by our expressions of love, and by our attitudes. "And may the Lord make your love for one another and for all people grow and overflow, just as our love for you overflows" (1 Thessalonians 3:12 NLT).

How Do We Grow in Love?

Over the coming week, take time each day to meditate on God's love for you and for others. Consider the ramifications of his great love on all that you do. Read Philippians 2:1–5.

Tell your family how much you love them and are thankful for them. Write them a note, or take time over a meal to speak to each of them individually about what they mean to you. If you need to apologize about anything, do it. If you need to make amends in some way or change the way you relate to any of them, start today. Read 1 Peter 3:7 and Ephesians 6:1–4.

Do you need to apologize to anyone in your past? Or forgive anyone? Message that person, make amends, and bring needed closure. Read Matthew 5:23–24.

Before you post online, consider: Does this sound loving from the other person's perspective? If you need to correct someone from time to time, can they tell you are doing it out of love? Also, think before posting a negative post. Read Proverbs 10:12 and 1 Corinthians 16:14.

How do you speak about other Christians? We are supposed to love the whole world, but especially our fellow followers of Christ. Consider how you talk about the church. Do you do it in a positive, encouraging, and loving way, so that people see your love for other Christians? Read John 13:34–35.

The Bible tells us God loves the world so much, He gave His only Son. Have you sensed God's great love for the world in your life? Pray that God will help you to love people who are different from you, and that He will give you more of His love for the world.

Pray and ask God to help you experience His love more deeply and to help you walk in greater love toward your family and friends.

CHAPTER 3

JOY

Though you have not seen him, you love him; and even though you do not see him now, you believe in him and are filled with an inexpressible and glorious joy, for you are receiving the end result of your faith, the salvation of your souls.

1 PETER 1:8—9

My friend Greg once took a ministry trip to Dallas. While there, out of curiosity, he began searching for cars online, looking specifically for the Green 1967 *Bullitt* Mustang. That was the infamous car driven by Steve McQueen in the movie *Bullitt* in what some have called the greatest car-chase scene of all time. Even with today's advances in film technology, no director has ever quite captured the excitement of that fourteen-minute car chase. To his delight, Greg found a replica of that car in Houston. So he made the trip over and ended up buying the car—without telling his wife until after the fact!

Ironically, this purchase led him to learn more of Steve McQueen's story. Greg had heard that McQueen had given his life to Christ before dying prematurely of cancer, but after church one day, a pilot who attended Greg's church pulled him aside and confided in him that he'd been the copilot on the final flight of Steve McQueen's life!

This led Greg on a several-year-long journey of research and interviews, and in the end he partnered with the Erwin Brothers to produce a documentary about McQueen's conversion, which was shown in theaters around the country. What started as an impulse purchase resulted in thousands of people hearing about the hope of the gospel through Steve McQueen's testimony.

McQueen had had a troubled childhood and youth. His mom had married and divorced several times, and his stepdads had been abusive. He was searching for something more. So

McQueen became an actor. His special style of acting usually stole the show, and he eventually became the highest paid actor in Hollywood, with more money than he knew what to do with. As a Hollywood bad boy, he lived on the edge with cool cars and fast women.

But after many years he felt unsatisfied. In the middle of his success, he left Hollywood, grew a beard, and hid out in northern California. Movie studios tried to reach him, offering him $50,000 just to read and consider a script. But he'd had enough of that life.

Instead, McQueen rented a small airplane hangar and began taking flying lessons, during which his flying instructor shared his faith in Jesus Christ with him and invited him to church. To everyone's surprise, McQueen began to go. One Sunday, while meeting with the pastor to ask some spiritual questions, McQueen told him that he had given his life to the Lord several Sundays before during the altar call.

Within a few years, McQueen died of cancer, but his journey makes an unforgettable statement about what really satisfies us in life. None of his wealth, opportunity, and notoriety could satisfy his heart, but when he came to faith in Jesus, he found the happiness and peace he'd been searching for. Even when he was diagnosed with cancer, he still had more joy in Jesus than he'd had before.

One of the exciting results of receiving Christ is joy. Many who make a decision to trust in Christ report a joy surging in their hearts, a joy they had longed for all their lives. Every other happiness doesn't last, is only momentary, and eventually leaves you wanting.

C. S. Lewis once wrote, "God cannot give us happiness

apart from himself, because it is not there—there is no such thing." God made you for Himself, and He has made a way for you to come to Him in Jesus. But it is up to each of us to trust in what He has done for us. The moment we trust Him, we receive the joy that we have been searching for our whole lives.

Lasting Happiness

Everyone is searching for lasting happiness. They look for it in success and achievement. They look for it in accumulating wealth. They look for it in social media likes and notoriety. They look for it in family, friends, and relationships. But happiness evades every heart that is void of Christ. Only Jesus can fill that hole in our hearts and give us lasting happiness.

This is not to say that joy is easy. There are many reasons you may struggle with finding joy, even as a Christian, and we'll talk about a few of them.

In Matthew 13, Jesus tells the story of a farmer sowing his seed. Sometimes the seed lands on the path and birds steal it away, by which Jesus meant that when some people hear the gospel, they don't understand it—the enemy steals away the message.

Sometimes the seed lands on shallow soil. This represents those people who initially might have heard the gospel with great joy, but their faith was shallow, and the joy didn't last. These people didn't stay connected to the source, so their joy diminishes as they move away from Christ.

Sometimes the seed grows up but soon is choked by weeds. This shows us what happens when our circumstances push us away from the joy we have in Jesus. He says that "the worries of this life and the deceitfulness of wealth choke the word." That is, in my humble opinion, the most common challenge for believers today who are struggling with joy. It's not that Jesus doesn't make us happy, but the worries and the concerns of life, the deceitfulness of things, pull us away from Christ; the deceitfulness of our own hearts causes us to walk off the path God wants for us; and all of this crowds out the happiness we have in Jesus.

Finally, some seed lands on good soil. Some people hear the Word of God, understand it, and it produces a bountiful harvest of good works throughout their lives, because of the great change Christ brings in their heart. Joy is essential in the life of a Christian. Philippians 4:4 beckons us, "Always be full of joy in the Lord. I say it again—rejoice!" (NLT). Joy is not a wavering promise, it is steady. It is we who waver. All of us struggle with joy at times, but we need to learn to walk in the joy Christ has promised us because genuine joy helps us represent Christ well to the world around us!

Let me add a disclaimer: we're not talking about some fake, pasted-smile-happiness that says everything is okay. The joy that comes from Christ is real, and deep, and anything but fake. Joy can be difficult. When you become a Christian, you bring a host of experiences into your new life, for the Bible warns us that our struggle with the old self will be a lifelong battle.

Consider these four realities that can affect your propensity for joy, your ability to find lasting happiness:

1. Your Personality Type
Depending on your personality type, you may be naturally more inclined to being outwardly happy, more subdued, more

hard-working, more compassionate, or so on. This reality may play into how you receive the fruit of the Spirit. Some of these traits will come more easily to you than others, and that's okay. But whatever your strengths and weaknesses, God wants to help you become more joyful, loving, kind, and gentle.

2. The Culture You Grew Up In

A non-Christian friend of mine in high school was kinder and more gracious than many people I knew, even some Christian friends at church. He was naturally a nice person. A number of factors may have played into his kindness, but one fact was that he grew up in a different part of the country, in a culture where people tended to be kinder and more considerate.

3. Your Heritage

Your family background may affect you more than any other factor. The way your parents interacted with you, the way they conveyed warmth, love, and security—or the lack of those things. How they treated each other can also affect you and your relationships for the rest of your life. Your attitudes today are deeply affected by your childhood; for instance:

- If your parents showed you what a true faith looks like, you are blessed.
- If your parents showed you what it looks like to be imperfect but still strive toward growth in grace, you are blessed.
- If your parents showed you what it looks like to go through hardship or challenge with a clear joy in the gospel, you are blessed.

This isn't to say you drew a bad straw if your parents set a negative example. Some of the most joyful Christians I know (my mom and grandmother-in-law, for instance) had poor examples in their parents, but God's grace has truly helped them overcome those circumstances. They trusted Christ to help them, and he has turned the tide for future generations of our family. Their examples have given me faith that Christ can change everything.

The Bible calls us to honor our parents, even if they have failed us significantly. Although it may be harder for you to honor your parents, that is often the first step toward new joy in Christ—when you submit to and obey God's Word, even when it's most difficult.

4. Mental Health

Some people struggle with joy because of mental health concerns. Clinical depression is real, and often the right medication can be invaluable. Yes, we should pray for God's healing power in our lives, but it's okay to take whatever appropriate medication the doctor prescribes. Even then, however, the points about joy raised in this chapter may be helpful.

Obstacles to Joy

If we are intentional, we can remove obstacles that hinder our joy. Consider these six factors that can hold us back from increasing our happiness:

1. Comparison

Social media has caused us to compare ourselves with others like never before. We see the best parts of people's lives flash constantly across the screen, which, according to one study, causes oxytocin to be released in our brains with the same intensity as getting married. Still, my friend, Dr. Sam Kim, a fellow at Harvard and Yale, has said that studies show "that Facebook is actually a mental health hazard. There is a direct link between clinical depression and Facebook usage. Why? Because, no one actually posts their bloopers, but only their highlights."[1] One thing is clear: we face a choice every time we scroll. Will we be happy for others' success, or will we give into comparison and wish for what others have?

When you scroll through social media, do you . . .

Judge people's happiness?

Wish for more likes and followers?

Wish your family was as happy as those in other people's pictures?

Wish for a different life?

Wonder if you are on the right track and pursuing the right things?

Envy others' success and opportunities?

If you said yes to any of these (I suspect 95 percent of us did), then comparison is a real issue for you. It's sapping your joy. It's a real problem in today's social-media-obsessed culture. Rather than being happy for what God has blessed us with, we become instantly dissatisfied with what we don't have, so we envy others. Comparison steals our joy.

We have to quit comparing the blooper reel of our life to the highlight reel of everyone else's. We have to realize that most people don't post their struggles on social media, and, when we're online, we have to be careful to have the mind of Christ, that is, we should celebrate with others in their wins and pray for God's blessings on everyone. The Bible says to "take every thought captive to obey Christ" (2 Corinthians 10:5 ESV). This includes not only sinful thoughts but our judgmental attitudes as we scroll through social media. How would Christ want us to think online? I believe He'd want us to be confident in the joy and blessings He's given us and not be swayed by others' success or opportunities. And I believe He'd want us to celebrate, pray for, and bless others.

The antidote to comparison and FOMO (the fear of missing out) is to remind yourself of what you've already been given in the gospel. You already have something greater than anything you could ever dream of. Your greatest dreams pale in comparison to what Jesus has done for you and what Jesus is preparing for you in heaven. You are a child of the King. The star-breathing God has called you by name. You are His. He has stamped you with His seal of approval, His Holy Spirit, and your life is now His. You have access to the throne of heaven because of what Christ has done. No matter what worldly achievements those on social media are posting about, you already have far more in the gospel!

If you fear you're missing out or if you're comparing yourself with certain friends, you may want to take some practical steps: temporarily snoozing or unfollowing certain people for a season can be liberating. Or you may want to take a break from social media altogether. You might try waiting until later in the day to get on social media, since this will keep you from stressing throughout the day about your comparisons to other people. Or you might want to keep a gratitude journal, in which you write down each simple joy that God has given you.

2. Fear and Uncertainty

My wife and I lost six of our relatives in a seven-year period. Some of those losses where due to old age, others were tragic and sudden. I'll never forget hearing about the death of one of our cousins in an automobile accident. The news wrecked our family. We wept together, and the pain still lingers many years later. Others, like my grandpa-in-law, passed peacefully in old age after a lifetime of ministry. He lived his life well. We were there as he passed into heaven, and the presence of God was evident.

Loss affects us all differently. If you've ever experienced the loss of a loved one, you know how much it can affect the rest of your life. Without God's grace in these situations, joy would be impossible. Sometimes the unexpected loss of a job can shake our world. Sometimes health problems or financial troubles undermine our confidence that God is with us and truly cares for us. My wife and I still get nervous when our parents call, because we're never quite sure whether they'll be reporting another unexpected loss. It's our new normal.

Loss leads to fear and uncertainty, which can hinder our joy, because we don't feel in control of our lives anymore. Ultimately, we have to learn to trust God's mercy and sovereignty in our lives. It's all too easy to base our joy on our successes, opportunities, wealth, or notoriety, but God calls us to a stronger and deeper joy that is based on His character and His care for us. We are called to live by faith.

Paul charged Timothy to "command those who are rich in this present world not to be arrogant nor to put their hope in wealth, which is so uncertain, but to put their hope in God, who richly provides us with everything for our enjoyment.

Command them to do good, to be rich in good deeds, and to be generous and willing to share" (1 Timothy 6:17–18). Wealth is uncertain. No matter how hard we work at our job, we will always have some level of uncertainty and, therefore, the continual need to trust God will care for us. He may not provide for all of our wants, but he promises to provide for all of our needs. He promises to "give you your heart's desires" if you "take delight in the LORD," and we know the God we serve is a God who "delights in every detail of our lives" (Psalm 37:4, 23 NLT). We can trust in Him to take better care of us than we could ever hope.

Every day you need to remind your heart to trust in God. David sang in the psalm, "Why, my soul, are you downcast? Why so disturbed within me? Put your hope in God; for I will yet praise him, my Savior and my God" (Psalm 43:5). Jesus told a powerful story in Matthew 7 about the fact that all of us are building our lives on the foundation of either rock or sand. He states as a fact that storms will come and that if we have built on rock, our house will stand strong. If we have built on sand, it will fall. The rock is hearing and following Jesus's teachings. Building on the rock means placing the foundation of our happiness on the gospel, on God's love for us, on what cannot be shaken. Everything in life could go wrong, but if we trust in Jesus, we have an unshakeable, eternal foundation and a grounded happiness—one that will not make sense to the world around us but may draw the world to what we have in Jesus.

3. Toxic Attitudes

Have you ever been around someone who drains your energy? Maybe that person is caught up in the world or gossips about others in a way that makes you uncomfortable. Maybe that person is someone you work with who never seems to be happy for or thankful for others. Toxic attitudes have a way of draining our joy and passion.

The people you work with or live near, those you interact with on a daily basis, can dampen or heighten your joy in life. Life is complex, but the people around us can diminish or enhance our propensity for joy. People who take more than they give drain our joy, and those who give more than they take fill us back up.

While you can't change other people, it can be helpful to ask yourself if *you* are the type of person who lifts up and encourages those around you.

You may find yourself in a season of caring for a parent who can't care for themselves, or you may find joy lacking in your marriage. In such situations, the answer is not to push others away, but to serve them, to endure those seasons, and to fervently ask God for renewed joy.

4. Busyness and Stress

How often do we lack joy simply because we burn the candle at both ends? We run ourselves ragged, never stop to rest, and wonder why we feel that way. Part of following Christ is learning to slow down, trust His help, and take needed breaks, knowing the world doesn't revolve around us. The weight of the world was never meant to be carried on our shoulders.

Busyness and stress go hand in hand, and life will not be lived with maximum joy until we learn to trust God and choose contentment. We have a part, and God has a part. We need to learn to trust Him and not try to go everywhere, do everything, and seize every opportunity. Instead, we need to incorporate rhythms of rest into our daily, weekly, monthly, and yearly schedules.

Maybe what you need is to take a day off, get more sleep, or spend a day celebrating with your family? That might be the path to joy for you. Consider how you can change your pace of life.

While stress can come through circumstances beyond our control, it can also come through circumstances we can control, like our lifestyle choices, poor nutrition or exercise, and other bad decisions. When we learn to honor God in all of these little areas of life, we will experience new joy. 1 Corinthians 10:31 addresses these areas: "So whether you eat or drink or whatever you do, do it all for the glory of God." We are called to honor God with our body. Sometimes you can't avoid stress, but a lot of our stress comes from poor decisions about our finances, schedules, nutrition, and so on. So let's recommit those to the Lord and recommit ourselves to the profound joy that's offered in the gospel.

5. Hardship

Joy is often dampened by discouraging situations, hardships, challenges in life, and even pain and suffering. My wife and I know a couple who went to Bible college around the same time we did. When the soon-to-be husband's three sisters were driving to the couple's wedding to participate as bridesmaids, they had a horrific traffic accident, and all three died. In a single moment, one of this couple's greatest joys in life was swept away in a flood of tragedy.

How do you recover after something like this? No way is

easy, but somehow, Christ has been their Rock, and they have carried on. Of course, their grief will always linger, but God graciously continues to work in them and give them joy even after unthinkable suffering. Their hope in the midst of grief is a testimony to everyone who knows them.

Maybe you have suffered the loss of a dream or the loss of hope over a struggle in your life. Perhaps you lost a spouse through divorce. Perhaps you lost a job that you loved. All those hardships can affect your capability for joy.

The good news is that Jesus can counteract those anxieties and wants to help you find new trust in Him and joy you wouldn't have been capable of on your own. David said, "When anxiety was great within me, your consolation brought me joy" (Psalm 94:19). The consolations of heaven can bring salve to our pain and heartache and can jumpstart new joy in our lives again. Keep pressing on to find the warm consolations that only God's Word can bring you.

6. Distance from Christ

Ultimately, much of our lack of joy comes when we grow distant from Christ. If you think about it, these six obstacles to joy become a subtle wedge between us and Christ. Ask yourself these questions:

- Is your busyness keeping you from time with the Lord or from church attendance?
- Has hardship or loss splintered your heart and kept you from trusting in the goodness of God?
- Are people with toxic attitudes distracting you from your peace and joy?

- Is the uncertainty of life keeping you from walking in steps of faith you know God has called you to take?
- Are you wishing for something more than what God has given you in the gospel, not realizing its amazing ramifications? Have you gotten stuck in comparing your life to someone else's rather than celebrating the gospel?

Too often we simply go through the motions of faith, without intimacy or interaction with God. We know about God, but we haven't sought Him out to truly know Him. Whether it's unrepentant sin in our lives, unforgiveness, or complacency about seeking God in His Word and in worship, our love for God has grown cold due to our own failure to really seek God.

The apostle John, exiled in old age to the Isle of Patmos, received the ground-shaking vision of Jesus that he wrote about in the book of Revelation. John heard Jesus's call to the churches of his day, a call that still rings true for Christians today: "I know your deeds, your hard work and your perseverance. I know that you cannot tolerate wicked people, that you have tested those who claim to be apostles but are not, and have found them false. You have persevered and have endured hardships for my name, and have not grown weary. Yet I hold this against you: You have forsaken the love you had at first. Consider how far you have fallen! Repent and do the things you did at first" (Revelation 2:2–5).

Do those words speak to you? Maybe you are steadfast in your faith, yet you have lost your deep love for the Lord and for other people. Maybe you have lost your joy somewhere along the way. God doesn't simply want us to stand strong in our faith, without evidence of the fruit of the Spirit. In Revelation, He calls us back to our first love, to do the things we did when we first came to faith in Christ.

Move away from whatever steals your joy in Christ, and move back toward your simple love for the Lord and for other people.

How to Get Your Joy Back

This list isn't comprehensive, but I hope it gets you thinking about what is stealing your joy and how you can get it back.

God Wants You to be Happy

Like a good parent, God wants us to be happy. He made the garden of Eden so we could walk in perfect nearness to Him, but our sin got in the way. Too many people think God doesn't want us to be happy. They believe He wants us to be holy but not happy.

But the Bible begs to differ. God calls you to be holy, and that holiness will be what makes you the happiest. He doesn't want you to get sidetracked by the "pleasures of sin" that will only last a short time and leave you unsatisfied, guilty, and broken. He wants to make you truly happy.

Sometimes we read the Bible out of guilt, but what if we read it as a road map to true joy? The Bible is a guide to the greatest joy we've ever known. God's commands are always for our good and His glory, and they lead us to a joy-filled, purposeful life.

In his book *60 Days of Happiness*, Randy Alcorn writes profoundly about the importance of realizing that God wants us to be happy. Happiness is something we all crave intuitively and will search for wherever we need to. The problem is, if the Church doesn't proclaim that happiness can be found in Christ, it will miss one of its greatest evangelistic tools.

In the King James Bible, the word *blessed* was used in those places where we would say *happy*. For instance, the Beatitudes in Matthew 5: "Blessed are the meek, for they will inherit the earth" means "Happy are the meek, for they will inherit the earth." For several hundred years, people understood that those words meant the same thing, but nowadays, the word *blessed* doesn't mean the same thing to people as happiness. God is truly happy and wants us to be truly happy. After all, the second fruit of the Spirit is joy!

This doesn't mean we should pursue whatever we think will make us happy. We should pursue God and the things of God, knowing that lasting happiness is found only in Him. God doesn't want us to lose our way by trying to find happiness in the things of this world, which will harm us or draw us away from Him. The things of this world will only leave us feeling empty.

But God wants you to be happy, and He shows you in His Word how to live a happy and joy-filled life. Joy is even one of the fruits of His Spirit. God's peace, salvation, grace, and hope can fill us with a happiness that the world can't give or take away. God cares about your happiness and wants to show you joy.

Celebrate Life

When did you last take a day off to celebrate life, love, and family? Life is too short not to celebrate milestones, celebrate your loved ones, and celebrate God's grace. You can celebrate birthdays, holidays, and maybe even special moments in your family's story, like a first day of school, golden birthday, family reunion, or any other days that are meaningful in unexpected ways. In my family, we go all-out in celebrating the kid's birthdays. It is powerful to build family traditions and rituals that you can look forward to every year.

We all need breaks and vacations. We all need to feel like we are more than a cog in a machine. We should fully engage in both rest and work. You don't want to live for the weekend, working a thankless nine-to-five job, but neither should we live for work. God has given us both work and rest for a reason, and we need both.

Practice Gratitude

Gratefulness multiplies joy. According to Harvard Medical School,

> Two psychologists, Dr. Robert A. Emmons of the University of California, Davis, and Dr. Michael E. McCullough of the University of Miami, have done much of the research on gratitude. In one study, they asked all participants to write a few sentences each week, focusing on particular topics.
>
> One group wrote about things they were grateful for. A second group wrote about daily irritations or things that had displeased them, and the third wrote about events that had affected them (with no emphasis on them being positive or negative). After 10 weeks, those who wrote about gratitude were more optimistic and felt better about their lives. Surprisingly, they also exercised more and had fewer visits to physicians than those who focused on sources of aggravation.[2]

Have you ever made a list of the things you're thankful for? This list should be a recurring practice in our lives. Let's not forget to be thankful for even the smallest blessings that God has given us. We should be a thankful people.

Ann Voskamp writes beautifully about gratefulness in her book *One Thousand Gifts*. In the midst of loss and pain, she began to make a list of a thousand little things she was grateful to God for. Starting that list changed her and filled her with joy. Starting a list like that could change you too. If you increase your gratefulness, you increase your joy.

A profound gratefulness should fill our lives as Christians. No matter what our circumstances happen to be, we know that the Son of God gave His life for us on the cross, and God will receive us in eternal joy one day.

Remember God's Eternal Promises

The eternal promises of the gospel meet us every day in practical ways and fill us with unshakeable hope. I have a friend who suffers from chronic pain and anxiety. When he considers the eternal promises of the Bible, he experiences a joy he wouldn't have any other way. One day, in heaven, he will have a new body. Freed from his body racked with pain, he will be released into enormous pleasure in God's presence forever. The gospel speaks to our everyday hardships and brings us joy in spite of our human frailty.

Paul's letter to the Ephesians describes many of the eternal promises we have because of Jesus. I've read Ephesians many times, but this year I began to study it deeply. Paul spends the first half of the letter (chapters 1–3) writing about the glory, wonder, and awe of the gospel. But he's writing from prison, under house arrest in Rome, uncertain of his future. Paul is talking about the glory of the gospel while he's suffering and imprisoned. As a pastor once told me, "The good news of the gospel is that despite your circumstances in this life, you get Jesus." I've heard it said that those who have suffered the most for their faith, those persecuted in countries closed off from the rest of the world, have experienced the deepest and most profound joy in Jesus. But no matter our circumstances in life and no matter what hardships we face, digging into the gospel can change us from the inside out. Just make sure you don't sit around in shallow faith like the seed that landed on rocky soil. Dig in.

The gospel contains countless eternal promises. These promises give us incredible hope and joy in Jesus no matter what happens. My friend Ryan Skoog and I set out to capture some of these epic promises in the gospel in our book *Chosen*, a thirty-day devotional about reminding your heart of the power of the gospel. That book shows what the power of the gospel can mean for our everyday life. We can never exhaust experiencing new joy when we meditate on the good news that saves us.

On the other hand, I knew a pastor who lost his job and began to work at a coffeehouse. I ran into him at a conference a few months into his new job, and he looked incredibly downcast and disappointed. We all feel this way at times, but I remember walking away thinking, "Where is his joy? There is a joy in the gospel, even in the loss of a job or a dream!" If temporary losses in this life make us lose our joy, we weren't placing our joy on the bedrock of the eternal promises of Christ.

Repent and Obey God

I have a friend who grew up in a ministry home. His dad was a pastor. He and his brothers also began to serve in ministry as adults. While serving as an executive pastor alongside his brother, my friend discovered that his brother was living a lie. His brother was guilty of several affairs, yet he felt he could simply continue in ministry. He tried to convince the leadership of the church to let his morality slide. My friend had to stand up to this error and courageously lead the church out of the mess it had become. My friend had no desire to hurt his brother, but he also couldn't let his brother continue to hurt the church, his family, and himself. As difficult as it was to walk through that, I saw in my friend's eyes the joy that comes from obedience to God.

My friend Greg Laurie has said, "This world says to find yourself. Jesus says to deny yourself, and follow Him, and you will find true life." If we are not careful, we will begin to believe the popular idea that we should follow our hearts. Matt Chandler warned against self-importance: "The more you actually walk in the belief that you're the sun and everyone else is the planets kind of orbiting around you, the more miserable of a human being you're going to be."[3] The Bible tells us our hearts are deceitful. Our fleeting emotions and sinful passions are not meant to be our guides. Instead, we need to do what the Bible says. We need to take up our cross daily and follow Jesus. Sometimes, what we want will be different than what God wants, and we will have to decide who we are following. Do we follow Jesus or ourselves? Jesus calls us to lay our opinions, emotions, passions, and decisions at the cross and to pick up the Christ-centered life.

We can't find lasting joy if we don't choose the way of Christ, and that way will always include denying ourselves. We must regularly lay down our opinions and believe God's Word instead, letting His Word change us and redirect us. That is how we carry our cross.

Denying ourselves starts with repentance. Pastor Choco De Jesus has said, "In our culture repentance has become a dirty word, but there is no refreshing and renewal without repentance."[4] Most often, new joy in Christ is found by confession, repentance, and turning from the sinful things that Christ calls us away from.

Joy comes from new obedience to God. The happiest life you can live is a life of following Jesus.

Forgive Anyone You Need To

One of the most incredible stories I've heard about the power of forgiveness comes from Corrie ten Boom. In Nazi Germany, Corrie's family came under fire for harboring Jewish people. Corrie and her sister were captured and taken to Ravensbruck concentration camp for concealing Jews. Her sister eventually died in that concentration camp from starvation. After the war was over, Corrie began sharing her story across Europe. On one particular night in Germany, she spoke on forgiveness. She told them that day that God throws our sins into the deepest ocean, and they are gone forever. A man came up to her after the service, and she quickly recognized him as one of the guards at the camp where she and many others had suffered so deeply. "You mentioned Ravensbruck in your talk. I was a guard there. It is so good to know God forgives me. I know God has forgiven me for the cruel things I did there, but would you be willing to forgive me also?"

> Betsie had died in that place. Could he erase her slow terrible death simply for the asking? I stood there with the coldness clutching my heart.

But forgiveness is not an emotion—I knew that too. Forgiveness is an act of the will, and the will can function regardless of the temperature of the heart.

"Jesus, help me!" I prayed silently. "I can lift my hand. I can do that much. You supply the feeling." And so woodenly, mechanically, I thrust my hand into the one stretched out to me.

And as I did, an incredible thing took place. The current started in my shoulder, raced down my arm, sprang into our joined hands. And then this healing warmth seemed to flood my whole being, bringing tears to my eyes. "I forgive you, brother!" I cried. "With all my heart!"[5]

Corrie saw the power of forgiveness after the war too. She again housed victims of the Holocaust in her home. Those who forgave their former enemies were able to rebuild their lives. Those that nursed their bitterness remained miserable.

If there is enough power for Corrie to forgive such an atrocity, then there is enough power for you to forgive too. When you forgive someone, you're not saying what they did is okay. You are simply entrusting the situation to God so your heart doesn't harbor bitterness anymore. And when you let go of your bitterness, you make way for joy.

Are there people that you need to forgive?

Because God has forgiven us such a great debt, we all need to forgive people who have sinned against us. As Jesus said, "For if you forgive other people when they sin against you, your heavenly Father will also forgive you. But if you do not forgive others their sins, your Father will not forgive your sins" (Matthew 6:14–15).

You will experience a breakthrough in your spiritual life if you forgive those who have hurt you, spoken ill of you, or sinned against you. This doesn't mean that you should let people walk all over you. Simply release their judgement into the hands of God, and trust that God will take care of you.

Walk in God's Purpose

There's an old saying: "If God called you to preach, don't stoop to be a king." Almost no one personifies that quote better than Billy Graham. Throughout his evangelistic ministry, people suggested he run for president of the United States. At other times he had some of the largest movie studios in Hollywood asking him to take on leading roles.

But Billy was not trying to say that being an evangelist is any better than other callings. His point was that God's calling *for you* is the most important thing *for you* to do. If God has called you to be a stay-at-home mom, do it with all your heart. If He has called you to teach or administrate at a local school, go for it. If you are called to start a business, run full steam ahead. Whatever your calling, know that it's more important than any other opportunity you could pursue. Success isn't about climbing a ladder, it's about stepping faithfully in the direction of what God puts on your heart to do. Life is short. Don't waste your life. Seek God for what He has put you on this earth for, and do that.

There is joy in knowing and following God's purpose for your life. Others might see it as unimportant or mundane, but you will experience the fullness of walking in what God has for you.

Maybe you are not on the right path. Maybe you are highly

successful, but you aren't sure if it's quite what God wants for you. Seek God's purpose for your life, and do whatever it takes to follow Him. When you know God has called you for a purpose, that's the most joyful life you can live.

Participate in Christian Community

Some of God's blessings only come through the local church. God has called us to and created us for community and unity with other Christians. Listening to a podcast or reading a Christian book isn't enough. We need to gather and worship with other believers. Corporate worship ignites our faith.

Do you find yourself going to church begrudgingly? Do you constantly critique every little thing at your church? I've had seasons in my life where I felt more critical than joyful about my church. I encourage you to press through that. Don't let negative seasons stop you from faithfully gathering for worship and God's Word. Hebrews warns us not to give up "meeting together, as some are in the habit of doing, but encouraging one another—and all the more as you see the Day approaching" (Hebrews 10:25). The encouragement of other believers brings joy to our walk.

Yet we can't simply sit in our church rows, staring at the backs of people's heads. We need rows, but we also need circles—like small groups. If you don't already, I'd recommend you start or join a small group. Small groups can enjoy meals together, do life together, and encourage and pray for each other. God wired us for close relationships, and these relationships will fill your heart with a joy you can't get anywhere else.

If you are not healthy enough to make it to church every week, this section is not meant to guilt you. Maybe you can find a group of believers that will meet with you in your home. Consider searching and praying for God to bring a group of believers into your life.

If you've been hurt by the church, as many have been, I encourage you to try again. I wish I could encourage and pray for you in person right now, that God may bring a different experience of the local church into your life. The body of Christ is big and diverse. I pray God opens your eyes to a new community of believers that can help heal your wounds and bless you more than you ever imagined!

Guard Margin

I've learned the hard way that there is a difference between time management and energy management. I may have time on my calendar and not have the energy because of how much I'm devoting to other people and projects. For example, I've realized that certain tasks deplete me more than others. For some reason, I do not like being on advisory boards of organizations. I've done this for a half dozen organizations and ministries over the years, but I've realized how much it depletes me. As good as those projects might be, I have to try not to take on projects that aren't the best fit for my God-given strengths and passions.

It's so easy to overfill our lives with good things. By overfilling our schedules, we lose sight of the best things. We walk around overwhelmed and stressed out, and it is usually by our own doing.

One of the best things we can do for our spiritual lives is to slow down and rest.

We should guard our margin. Our margin is the time we

have without outside responsibility. Margin is good for our finances, our schedules, and our workload. How often do we use every spare minute checking our phones? We are a generation who doesn't know how to give ourselves margin. Here are some ways to guard your margin:

- Say no to some things. This allows you to focus on the things God has called you to. Otherwise, you will get distracted and overwhelmed.
- Don't spend your entire paycheck every month. A good rule of thumb is to give 10 percent to the Lord and 10 percent to savings.
- Take short breaks in between projects throughout your workday to think, rest, or pray.
- Take at least one day off every week.
- Be careful how many sports or extracurricular activities you put your kids in. Don't let those things crowd out your family's commitment to church or ability to rest.
- Finish your work at a reasonable time every evening. Some people will always have more work than they can handle. Learn to put it down for another day.
- Turn off "work mode" when you come home to be with your family. Learn when to put your screens away, and when to turn off the work conversation, and simply enjoy life together. Have a life outside of your work.
- Take time daily to read God's Word, pray, and worship. This is the biggest margin reset you can do. It will transform your life and keep you on the right track.
- If possible, schedule a week of vacation.

Stay Connected with Christ

God develops us in the fruit of the Spirit as we are connected to Him. As Jesus taught, if we abide in Him, we will bear much fruit. The fruitfulness of our lives is determined by our connectedness to Christ. So make sure you keep reconnecting.

Some ways that we connect with Christ are:

- Reading and meditating on the Word of God. It only takes about ten minutes a day to read through the Bible every year. As D. L. Moody said, "I never saw a fruit-bearing Christian who was not a student of the Bible."[6]

- Prayer and worship. The foundation of the Christian life is worship. We were created for it. Worship fills our lives with the presence of God. Pray for what you need. Thank God for all He has done, especially for the cross and resurrection. And be sure to pray for others, and not just your own needs.

- Church attendance and Christian community. We were not meant to live on our own. Scripture says that God is near when we gather in worship.

- Obedience. Is there an area of your life where you haven't been obeying God? All the Bible study, prayer, and church attendance in the world won't fix your problem if you aren't obeying God. Turn from sin, and turn to God. Joy will come every time.

Walking in Joy Will Give You Influence

God wants you to be joyful. Jesus gives us a joy this world cannot give or take away.

Genuine joy helps us influence others for the sake of the gospel. Robert Chapman once said, "Our joy speaks a language that all hearts can understand. Our joy is a testimony for God."[7] When we remove obstacles to joy in Jesus and lean into the joy He wants for us, people will want to be around us and be like us. Our joy will help people see the benefits of the gospel.

Many years ago I preached in Duluth, Minnesota. The church was on a hillside overlooking Lake Superior. After the service, my friend and I noticed a man staring in awe as people came out of the service. We greeted him and asked how he was doing. He said, "Just look at all those people. They are so happy." We took the opportunity to share the gospel with him! In the same way, your joy in Jesus will draw other people to you and give you an opportunity to influence them in both truth and love and to point them to the Source of your joy.

So I pray this along with Paul for you: "May the God of hope fill you with all joy and peace as you trust in him, so you may overflow with hope by the power of the Holy Spirit" (Romans 15:13).

How Do We Grow in Joy?

In the coming week, set aside some time of rest, to celebrate life and grow in happiness. Remember that God wants you to be truly happy.

Make a list of fifty things you are thankful for, and don't forget to pray and thank God for His many blessings in your life.

Tell someone special in your life how much they mean to you.

Consider if the attitude you have at work and with family is joyful. If not, what are some practical ways you can begin to grow in this area?

Ask God to help you experience joy, especially with your family and friends.

CHAPTER 4

PEACE

I have told you these things, so that in me you may have peace. In this world you will have trouble. But take heart! I have overcome the world.

JOHN 16:33

It was a balmy, humid day as I drove to a church near our hotel. I met with a group of two dozen journalists and ministry leaders to talk about a major motion picture that was being filmed nearby. Our ministry has had the opportunity to help a few faith-based films tell their story and extend their impact, and this has led to some unique opportunities to visit movie sets and Hollywood red carpet events. The movie we were helping with on that sunny day has a fascinating backstory.

Universal Studios bought the "life rights" to Louis Zamperini's story nearly seventy years ago. But the lead actor Universal wanted to play Zamperini was cast in another film, and the project got sidelined for nearly fifty years. During the 1998 Winter Olympics in Nagano, Japan, Zamperini's story resurfaced, and Laura Hildebrand began writing his story in her book *Unbroken*.

Louis spent most of his life under difficult circumstances. He was a rebellious teenager, always getting into trouble, but eventually he straightened up his act. He began to achieve national recognition for being one of the youngest runners at the Berlin Olympics in 1936. He has been called one of the greatest middle-distance runners of his time. He was a hopeful for gold in the 1940 Olympics, however it was called off after the start of World War II. This resulted in him enlisting in the Army Air Corps in 1941.

Zamperini and his crew had survived on a life raft on the

open ocean for weeks after their plane crashed during a routine drill. The Japanese discovered them, and Zamperini suffered under brutal conditions as a Japanese prisoner of war for nearly two years. He returned home as a war hero.

After the war, PTSD and alcoholism haunted him. They continued to take their toll as he met and fell in love with his soon-to-be wife. Their romance struggled as his drinking grew and his inner demons continued to torture him.

Around the same time, a young evangelist by the name of Billy Graham and his small ministry team had been setting up a Los Angeles crusade. In September 1949, near downtown Los Angeles, Billy Graham began his historic LA crusade, which catapulted him into the national and international spotlight, eventually opening the doors for him to share the gospel of Jesus Christ to millions around the globe.

Louis Zamperini's wife attended that crusade and eventually gave her heart to the Lord. At the time, her and Louis's marriage was struggling. They had a young daughter, but Louis's pain, anger, and alcoholism had only grown. His wife told him she would divorce him unless he attended the Billy Graham crusade. Louis attended, but night after night he left angry. That is, until one night the gospel opened his heart to the peace of God, and in a single moment he was set free from his alcoholism and PTSD. In fact, his heart opened in such an amazing way that he started looking for a way to return to Japan to forgive his captors, especially the man who had cruelly and mercilessly beat him night after night for two years.

When Universal finally made a movie about Zamperini, Angelina Jolie directed and acted in the film, which was also titled *Unbroken*. She was captivated by his inner strength. How could he forgive those who had done so much evil? Where did his inner strength come from? Jolie directed the film, which told the first part of Zamperini's story. Now Universal, along with several other studios, has greenlit a sequel. This second film explores Zamperini's faith journey. He was not truly unbroken until he met Jesus at that Billy Graham crusade in 1949.

I had the opportunity to hear the story firsthand from his son Luke. Luke suspected that he would not have even been born if his father had not met Christ. Something happens in a person when the gospel is heard, understood, and received. There is a peace that envelops the heart and mind. Louis experienced a peace that set him free from the nightmare of PTSD, restored his relationship with his wife and children, and started him on God's path for his life, helping delinquent youth and sharing the gospel.

Billy Graham preached a similar message all over the world throughout his ministry, and possibly even on the night that Louis Zamperini put his faith in Jesus Christ: "The only way to lasting peace is through faith in Jesus Christ."[1]

Why did Jesus come? Because there is no peace without Him. We long for peace, but we can't find lasting peace outside of faith in Christ. When we accept the gospel, our hearts are flooded with peace, sometimes immediately. Jesus permeates our lives with peace. This peace is first and foremost peace with God, and our peace with God infiltrates and restores peace in other areas of our lives.

The Bible speaks often about this incredible peace with God. The Bible also calls us to walk in peace with the world around us. We should consider these two areas of peace: inner peace and peace with others. One is freely given in the gospel.

And every Christian who has received God's peace is called to constantly work in God's strength toward the other.

God Gives Us Inner Peace

Why do we need peace with God? The Bible actually tells us we used to be enemies with God until Christ saved us through His death and resurrection.

When you read the Bible, you see that humanity's propensity toward sin and idolatry is indefatigable. Over and over, we go the wrong way. God works to reconcile us and shows us incredible grace, yet we reject His grace and turn away. This is why God sent His Son: to pay the penalty of our waywardness and to give His Spirit to work within our hearts to help us follow Him. When we believe in and receive the truth, Jesus does an amazing work in us.

Jesus wants to give us inner peace. "Peace I leave with you; my peace I give you. I do not give to you as the world gives. Do not let your hearts be troubled and do not be afraid" (John 14:27). He doesn't give us some generic sense of peace; He gives us His own peace! There should be a sense of a peace in our lives that doesn't quite make sense to us. It's otherworldly. It's the peace of Christ.

There are moments in our Christian lives when we feel more anxiety than peace. In those moments, the Bible calls us back to the peace of God. "Do not be anxious about anything, but in every situation, by prayer and petition, with thanksgiving, present your requests to God. And the peace of God, which transcends all understanding, will guard your hearts and your minds in Christ Jesus" (Philippians 4:6–7). God's peace will guard our hearts and minds, and his peace will be beyond our understanding.

We get back to God's peace by steadfastly trusting in God and His care for us, even in the messiness of life. "You will keep in perfect peace those whose minds are steadfast, because they trust in you" (Isaiah 26:3). Do you need more of God's peace in your life? Come back to childlike trust in God's care for you. "Let the peace of Christ rule in your hearts" (Colossians 3:15), and "Cast all your anxiety on him because he cares for you" (1 Peter 5:7).

Jesus also said that this peace would be present even in the midst of the problems of the world. He did not say we wouldn't have trouble. He actually warned us that there would be challenges to our faith and to our peace but that we could find unshakeable peace in Him. "I have told you these things, so that in me you may have peace. In this world you will have trouble. But take heart! I have overcome the world" (John 16:33).

Christians can be calm in a crazy world. These days people tend to wring their hands at every announcement of bad news. This culture of outrage has infiltrated our churches. But as believers, we are supposed to have hope! If we act like there is no hope, we are subtly signaling to the world that there isn't anything different about us. Instead, we need to walk with a peace that doesn't make sense to the world around us. Doing so will give us influence for the sake of the gospel. Christians can have an overwhelming and pervasive sense of well-being no matter what else is going on.

God Reigns over the Chaos

God is writing the story of our world, even the story of our world's leaders (Proverbs 21:1; Daniel 2:21; Romans 13:1). God's sovereignty won't always make sense to us, but the truth of God's sovereignty should serve to remind us the world will never spin out of God's control. God is not surprised when the world rages (Psalm 2:1–6).

This doesn't mean humanity doesn't have responsibility, but that God is ultimately Sovereign. Have you ever considered how much of the pain and suffering in the world is caused by humans willfully pursuing selfish or sinful desires? How much of this could be avoided if we would obey God? Chaos in our world doesn't prove God isn't there, it just proves how much we need to invite God into our world.

J.I. Packer has written, "The stars, indeed, may fall, but God's promises will stand and be fulfilled."[2] Our world may seem beyond repair, but God is always working for those who wait for Him. Tragedy will always rise up, but we Christians will always rise up to bring the hope and love of God to the hurting.

We Know How Our Story Ends

The Bible tells us how our story will end when we trust in Christ: in heaven forever with God. As Pastor Eric Geiger has written, "God has designed the end *and* the means. The end is people from every tribe, tongue, and nation gathered around the throne worshipping Him because they were purchased with the blood of Christ (Rev. 5:9–10). Regardless of what happens this week, what unfolds in the news, the ending has already been made clear: God is redeeming for Himself a people from all peoples."[3]

Our hope is not an earthly hope. It is eternal. No matter

what we face in this life, we are heading to perfect joy with God forever. We can find real peace in that.

They Will Know We Are Christians by Our Love

In *The Mark of a Christian*, Francis Schaeffer shares powerfully about how the Bible calls Christians to walk in love toward each other. People can see our love in the way we act in peace with one another. Are we constantly squabbling? When we have disagreements, do we converse in love? Can the world see the difference in us, even in the way we argue?

We need to be careful to show each other honor, even in our disagreements. Living peacefully in our disagreements with other Christians shows the world that the peace Christ gives us is unique and can draw them to our hope.

Unity Does Not Mean Uniformity

Jesus prayed His Church would be one. He was praying for a peace and unity between His followers around the world, so they would represent Him well to the watching world.

We don't have to agree on everything in order to show others respect and dignity.

My friend Bobby Schuller shared an example of this a while back. Bobby saw two people bickering and disagreeing about something, and then they politely agreed to disagree. He teasingly added, "Oh, they must have been Canadians."

But shouldn't Christians be that way? What if when we disagreed, we did so with such love and respect that people immediately responded, "Oh, they must be Christians."

Unity doesn't mean uniformity. We can live in unity and respect for each other despite our differences. We are called to honor each other and strive toward peace and true Christlike love.

People Don't Care How Much You Know until They Know How Much You Care

We are called to be peacemakers, not to add our voices to the world's chaos. This can be very difficult when we see the world burning itself down with bad ideas. There are times to speak truth, but if we sound like the world when we do speak, we will lose our ability to influence people. We ought to disagree differently. When we disagree, people should be able to tell how much we care for them and see our respect for them and the fruit of the Spirit in us. Sometimes we need to love others enough to tell them we disagree, but we need to do that with care.

James and John responded like most Christians today, but Jesus wasn't having it:

> Jesus resolutely set out for Jerusalem. And he sent messengers on ahead, who went into a Samaritan village to get things ready for him; but the people there did not welcome him, because he was heading for Jerusalem. When the disciples James and John saw this, they asked, "Lord, do you want us to call fire down from heaven to destroy them?" But Jesus turned and rebuked them. (Luke 9:51–55)

There's incredible power in the gospel. Though Jesus could've called down fire from heaven, His focus was on teaching them about a new kingdom of peace, love, and gentleness.

Jesus did say some strong words to religious leaders a few times. But most of His ministry was characterized by incredible compassion and love, even though He had always maintained the authority to speak even stronger. He is a picture of God's gentleness, walking in truth and love. Yes, Jesus flipped over tables in the temple, but only once. So, I like to tell fellow Christians that they can flip the tables too, but only once in their lifetime!

Peace in Your Relationships

"As far as it depends on you, live at peace with everyone" (Romans 12:18). Does this exclude people you disagree with? Does this only pertain to people who share your political views? It often takes greater courage to be a person of peace, than to speak your mind and try to have the last word. Maybe, at the appropriate time, our silence can show the world a different side of courage, that we can be people of peace among differing worldviews. Another Scripture passage tells us to "make every effort to live in peace with everyone and to be holy; without holiness no one will see the Lord" (Hebrews 12:14). Make every effort. What can you do to walk in greater peace with others? Take those small steps to hold your tongue, forgive, or apologize when you need to. This leads to a life of greater and greater peace.

Blessing, Not Cursing

Scripture says, "Do not repay evil with evil or insult with insult. On the contrary, repay evil with blessing, because to this you were called so that you may inherit a blessing. For 'Whoever would love life and see good days must keep their tongue from evil and their lips from deceitful speech. They must turn from evil and do good; they must seek peace and pursue it'" (1 Peter 3:9–11). We are not called to respond to the world in the same way they speak to us. We are called to have a different spirit. We should bless others, not insult them. Our mouths were meant to be used for blessing God, not cursing people (James 3:9–10). It's better to light a candle than curse the darkness. We don't fight darkness with darkness. We must be people who praise God and say praiseworthy things.

Don't Respond to Everything

"Even fools are thought wise if they keep silent, and discerning if they hold their tongues" (Proverbs 17:28). There is godly wisdom in not responding to everything in our culture. We should have the discipline to hold our tongues and our social media posts and not say everything that comes to our minds. Have you recently responded to someone too quickly or harshly? How can you respond in peace next time? Are there times when you should not respond at all?

Focus on What Is Praiseworthy

In Philippians 4:8–9, God's peace is not given by default, but by directing our thoughts to what is true, pure, and praiseworthy: "Finally, brothers and sisters, whatever is true, whatever is noble, whatever is right, whatever is pure, whatever is lovely, whatever is admirable—if anything is excellent or praiseworthy—think about such things. Whatever you have learned or received or heard from me, or seen in me—put it into practice. And the God of peace will be with you." When we exhibit self-control, and don't let culture flood our thoughts with fear and worry, we can better direct our thoughts in a way that leads to greater peace.

When Christians watch our culture of outrage yet don't feel the need to speak to all of it, it can reveal God's glory:

- Instead, we lament, weep, and pray, simply trusting the One who is sovereign to work on our behalf in the midst of it all.
- Instead, we are people of a different kingdom, letting the darkness of our time cause our light to shine even brighter.
- Instead of hate, we promote love. Instead of cutting words, we show honor to all.

We may need to start by muting those voices and media that stir up our anger. We were made to live in the peace of God, not in toxic conditions. Shut off the cable news, unfollow online accounts that stir up anger, and avoid unhelpful political arguments at family gatherings that lead to anger. Open the Word of God instead, and let God's peace invade your weary soul.

It's worth noting that Jesus and the apostles did not spend the majority of their time speaking against the Roman government, which was deeply corrupt. They focused on preaching the gospel because only the truth of Jesus can change hearts and the world. Early church leaders honored and prayed for those in authority, and this allowed Christians to influence kings. We can't let the powerful message of the gospel and God's call to honor all people get sidetracked by momentary culture wars.

Again, there may be times to speak up about culture, but always in the way Jesus would do it.

God calls us to walk in His peace, not add our voices to the world's chaos. Now this doesn't mean we shouldn't speak truth (even when it's unpopular). When we do need to speak the truth in our culture, our tone, motivations, and heart should be the opposite of this world. We should have the tone of peacemakers.

May you experience God's profound peace in your life today, and may you become a peacemaker toward others around you. "Now may the Lord of peace himself give you peace at all times and in every way. The Lord be with all of you" (2 Thessalonians 3:16).

How Do We Grow in Peace?

Over the coming week turn off your TV, and stop your news notifications. Take just one week to not focus on what is wrong with the world, and simply enjoy your life.

Is there someone you need to forgive or apologize to? Take time over the next few days to forgive or apologize to them.

Consider your words over the coming week. Are your words adding to the world's chaos, or are they representative of God's peace and His call to be a peacemaker with others?

Pray and ask God to help you know His peace and to be a peacemaker toward others, especially those you disagree with.

CHAPTER 5

KINDNESS AND GENTLENESS

Be kind to one another, tender-hearted, forgiving each other, just as God in Christ also has forgiven you.

EPHESIANS 4:32 NASB

"But how is it that Christians can simply 'roll over' when conflict hits?"

I had the opportunity to do a ministry podcast interview a few years back, and this question came at me over the phone. I was sharing my heart for Christians to walk in the fruit of the Spirit, in kindness and gentleness, and the pastor interviewing me seemed surprised. He felt that Christians need to tell people the truth and that the truth is sometimes harsh. Do we really need to be gentle? My response was that gentleness is a fruit of the Spirit. We are walking in the flesh, not the Spirit, whenever we are not gentle and kind. We are walking in God's way when our words and responses, even in speaking difficult truths, are full of kindness and gentleness.

It's amazing how even some well-known ministry leaders struggle to understand this biblical concept. We can be really good at pounding home the truth, but we struggle to pound home kindness and gentleness, especially in our own lives. Kindness is likely more of a struggle for driven leaders and leaders who are passionate about defending God's truth.

Christians talk a lot about love, but I don't hear very much talk about kindness and gentleness. Kindness and gentleness seem like forgotten fruits of the Spirit. What if, in our churches and small groups, we spent time considering and discussing how we can live in kindness and gentleness?

If I were to sum up kindness and gentleness (and maybe all the fruit of the Spirit) in one word, it might be graciousness.

How is the world supposed to see the grace of God if Christians are not gracious? When we walk in kindness and gentleness, it helps people see God's grace.

When you read the Bible's many commands to be gentle, compassionate, kind, and humble, you cannot help but wonder how a Christian can act passionately about the Bible and yet act ungraciously. We have to be cautious about being passionate about our favorite parts of the Bible and not others. If we want to be passionate about the truth of God's Word, we must be passionate about kindness and gentleness.

The biblical Epistles all seem to have a similar flow. They start with an epic, cosmic picture of God's glory and then essentially tell us to be nice. Nowadays, *nice* has a bad rap as something spineless, lifeless, and bland. As we look to the Gospels, we see an entirely different picture, in which niceness, or kindness, is potently countercultural. The flow is like this: God is glorious, amazing, incredible, and has given us so much in the gospel . . . so walk in kindness and gentleness! Of course, the Gospels contain calls to other areas of holiness as well.

Listen to some passages and commands of Scripture about this, with some short notes from me following each Scripture. Read it slowly if you need to. This may be like a spiritual carwash for some of you. Others may need to weep in repentance as you read through this list. For still others, you may sense you are on the right track:

Forgive Others like God Forgives You

"Be kind to one another, tenderhearted, forgiving one another, as God in Christ forgave you" (Ephesians 4:32 ESV). C. S. Lewis has said, "To be a Christian means to forgive the inexcusable, because Christ has forgiven the inexcusable you."[1] According to Scripture, we should be forgiving, kind, and gentle because God has been that way with us. We need to follow Jesus's way of influence.

Reconcile Your Broken Relationships

"Therefore, if you are offering your gift at the altar and there remember that your brother or sister has something against you, leave your gift there in front of the altar. First go and be reconciled to them; then come and offer your gift" (Matthew 5:23–24). If you have spewed critical words and left broken relationships strewn throughout your life and think you can simply move on and follow Jesus, you're wrong. Jesus tells you to stop coming to the altar to seek God as if everything's okay. First, go apologize and make amends. Then you will truly be seeking and experiencing God.

Let Kindness and Gentleness Be Evident in Your Life

"Therefore, as God's chosen people, holy and dearly loved, clothe yourselves with compassion, kindness, humility, gentleness and patience" (Colossians 3:12). We "clothe ourselves" with these traits of kindness, gentleness, and compassion toward other people. We wear them out in public for others to see. These should be visible traits in our lives as Christians. Kindness and gentleness should define us to the world around us. Christians have become known more for what they are against than for what they are for. We need to do our best to become known more for kindness and gentleness than for our protests. Micah 6:8 says, "He has told you, O man, what is good; and what does the LORD require of you but to do justice, to love kindness, And to walk humbly with your God?" (Micah 6:8 ESV). Do you love kindness? If we don't seek justice, love kindness, and walk humbly with God, we are missing the heart of God. If you're not known for your kindness, you need to take a good look at this Scripture again.

Look Different than the World

"Don't repay evil for evil. Don't retaliate with insults when people insult you. Instead, pay them back with a blessing. That is what God has called you to do, and he will bless you for it" (1 Peter 3:9 NLT). We are not called to live as the world lives or respond as the world responds. We are called to be a people of blessing, not cursing (Romans 12:14). Let's ask God to help us make this the culture of our hearts.

Corrupting Talk Has No Place in Our Lives

"Let no corrupting talk come out of your mouths, but only such as is good for building up, as fits the occasion, that it may give grace to those who hear" (Ephesians 4:29 ESV). How much corrupting talk are we allowed? How much criticism and harshness? None! When we speak out of line with God's call for us, we must repent. As Christians, our words should build people up and give grace. Think through your social media posts lately, your comments with coworkers, or your conversations with your spouse. How much time do you spend complaining about problems or politics? Do you regularly belittle the Christian church? God told us to turn from corrupting talk and to focus on building others up in grace.

Paul warned Timothy about it too. "Don't get involved in foolish, ignorant arguments that only start fights. A servant of the Lord must not quarrel but must be kind to everyone, be able to teach, and be patient with difficult people. Gently instruct those who oppose the truth. Perhaps God will change those people's hearts, and they will learn the truth" (2 Timothy 2:23–25 NLT). We have to be careful how we argue as believers. We are called to be people of peace, kindness, and gentleness. Elsewhere, the Bible compares hypocrisy and deceitfulness to unkind speech.[2] Many Christians are adamantly against hypocrisy and deceitfulness, but think unkind speech is acceptable. Kindness isn't an extracurricular trait that would be nice to have; it is an indispensable trait God commands us to walk in.

A Worthy Walk Is Kind and Gentle

Paul wrote to the church in Ephesus, "As a prisoner for the Lord, then, I urge you to live a life worthy of the calling you have received. Be completely humble and gentle; be patient, bearing with one another in love. Make every effort to keep the unity of the Spirit through the bond of peace" (Ephesians 4:1–3). Paul reminds them that he is as spiritual as anyone, since he is in prison for the gospel. And then, rather than calling them to be culture warriors and free him, he asks them to be completely humble and gentle. Not the words you expect to hear, but this is the way of Christ. Bear with others. Keep the unity of the Spirit. He wrote to the church in Philippi saying, "Let your gentleness be evident to all" (Philippians 4:5). Is your gentleness evident to all or just to the people you agree with politically? Even if we think another Christian is off base or even if we know someone is living in sin, we should work in gentleness toward their restoration, not their defeat (see Galatians 6:1). Jesus encouraged his disciples to learn from His humble and gentle heart (see Matthew 11:29).

Be Kind to Difficult People

Paul writes, "Remind the people to be subject to rulers and authorities, to be obedient, to be ready to do whatever is good, to slander no one, to be peaceable and considerate, and always to be gentle toward everyone" (Titus 3:1–2). Paul has Titus's attention to bring a word to the church, and his message is simple. Slander no one. Be considerate. Walk in peace and gentleness!

We Gain Influence through Kindness and Gentleness

"Whoever pursues righteousness and love finds life, prosperity and honor" (Proverbs 21:21). There are benefits to being nice. Sometimes being nice gets a bad rap, but walking in kindness and righteousness brings benefits. You have a greater influence with people. People think more highly of you if you treat them with honor. Some translations (like the ESV) replace the word *love* with *kindness*. Walking in kindness with others can truly bless you.

How do you feel after reading all those Scriptures? We could have read many more.[3] Do you see how kindness and gentleness can get lost in our Christian subculture and why we need to get them back? Our heavenly Father has shown us extraordinary kindness, and He wants us to represent Him to the world, so the world may come to know His love. Walking in kindness and gentleness is a holy task indeed.

Obstacles to Kindness and Gentleness

We are not without obstacles to living a life of kindness and gentleness. Here are eight common ways that Christians bypass the call of Christ to kindness and gentleness.

Our World Is Harsh

Because the world around us can be so harsh and angry, we can feel we have every right to act this way. But God calls us to be different from the world, to be "set apart."

We all struggle with kindness and gentleness. It is a daily struggle for me. I have to resubmit my attitudes to the Lord, and sometimes I have to apologize to my wife or kids for my behavior.

A lot of times when I get angry at my kids, I realize I'm not even upset about something they've done, and some stress at work is what is really eating away at me. I'm worried about the future, or I experienced something harsh, so I end up responding in anger. Not until I look into my heart, remember what is stressing me out, and process it in a proper way can I let go of my harsh feelings. To process my feelings, I remind myself that God has always been faithful and that He will help me and provide for me. I might offer my concern in prayer to the Lord, asking

Him to give me peace. Usually He calms my fears, and I tend to act a bit more graciously to those around me.

Maybe your parents or other people you looked up to have been harsh or demeaning, and you've picked up these traits from them. Shaking a habit can take time, but never lose sight of what God calls you to—to treat those closest to you with kindness and gentleness.

Really, I think we need to focus on kindness and gentleness with the people closest to us. If you are married, start with your spouse. If you are a parent, consider how you can be gentler with your kids. If you are single, consider how you can be gentler with a roommate, close friends, or coworkers.

Having a Critical Spirit

Some people are critical of everything. We've all experienced people like this. One time I posted a Bible verse on my Facebook profile about helping the poor, and several people found a way to pick that apart because they assumed I had some sort of political motivation. I hope they understood they were arguing with God, not me.

The Billy Graham Evangelistic Association has a wonderful evangelism training that we've used over the years at some of our conferences. In one section, they warn Christians against the four *d*'s: being demeaning, demanding, domineering, or dogmatic. The solution to the four *d*'s is to make sure we are walking in kindness and gentleness.

D. L. Moody once said, "The only way any church can get a blessing is to lay aside all criticism, coldness, and division, and come to the Lord as one."[4] How do we bypass God's blessing on our life, family, church, or community? Walking in criticism, coldness, and division. How do we receive God's blessing? Repent and walk in kindness, warmth, and peace!

Being Overly Intense

Sadly, we could pray for hours, steep ourselves in the Bible, fast rigidly, sound hyperspiritual in how we talk, and still be a jerk. It shouldn't be this way, but the reality is that spiritual maturity isn't always what it seems.

We tend to think that Christians who are the most intense or austere are the most spiritually mature. I spent a great deal of my life thinking that way. I've slowly realized that true Christlikeness looks a whole lot more like kindness and gentleness than how many big spiritual words we know, how intense we are, or how much we fast or read our Bible.

Spiritual disciplines like prayer, Bible reading, and fasting are important. They can refine us spiritually, build our faith, and help us be more like Jesus. However, these disciplines don't automatically mean we will grow the way God wants us to be, unless we receive biblical teaching to help open our eyes to what God really wants.

James 3:13, 17 says, "If you are wise and understand God's ways, prove it by living an honorable life, doing good works with the humility that comes from wisdom. . . . The wisdom from above is first of all pure. It is also peace loving, gentle at all times, and willing to yield to others. It is full of mercy and the fruit of good deeds. It shows no favoritism and is always sincere" (NLT).

My father-in-law is a great example of what James is talking about. My father-in-law is deeply spiritual, but he doesn't feel the need to prove it at every turn. Instead, he shows it through his attitude and his humility. For example, when he followed in his own father's footsteps and began to pastor at our church, he sensed God calling him to be a transitional leader. Even though he was celebrated and could've pastored for many years, he felt the Lord nudging his heart to make room for the next lead pastor after eleven years of service, so he humbly transitioned out, not needing power or influence to make him feel significant. He knows how to lead well, but he also knows how to rest and take a step back so others can lead.

The Bible encourages us to grow in spiritual maturity, becoming more like our Savior. Spiritual maturity is not intense, hyperspiritual talk. It is pure, peaceful, considerate, submissive, merciful, and sincere.

Too Much News Media

Nowadays, one of the biggest culprits to our unkindness is the media we watch or listen to. Highly politicized news media barrages the heart and mind with negativity, fear, and cynicism and has helped create the divisive culture we live in today.

The Bible tells us instead to focus our minds on "whatever is true, whatever is noble, whatever is right, whatever is pure, whatever is lovely, whatever is admirable—if anything is excellent or praiseworthy" (Philippians 4:8). Most news media focuses our minds on the opposite, stirring up our anxieties, anger, and outrage.

I am not saying we need to bury our head in the sand. But consider that no other generation has had the type of twenty-four-hour, negative news cycle media that we have today. Pastor Dave Ferguson points out that just one email from the *New York Times* contains more information than someone two centuries ago was likely to encounter in their lifetime.[5]

Get your news when you need to, but be watchful over your mind and heart. Don't simply become a parrot for your preference of news media. We need to be rooted in the hope of God's Word more than we complain about the state of the world. Yes, lament and protest are appropriate at times, but those shouldn't overtake our primary message of hope.

Too Little Margin

A psychology study was done in the 1970s that set up seminarians in a similar situation to the Bible story of the Good Samaritan. The study found that seminary students who had extra time before they needed to turn in their paper were far more likely to be a Good Samaritan to a staged homeless man on the way to their professors' office than students who were running late.[6] Margin and being unrushed go a long way to help us walk in kindness, gentleness, and the rest of the fruit of the Spirit.

If we don't have margin in our finances or schedules, we tend to be far more irritable. For example, if you usually leave for work without accounting for rush-hour traffic, how do you react when somebody cuts you off in traffic? Whereas, if you give yourself extra time to get to work, you will be far less likely to blow up when somebody slows you down.

It might not sound like a spiritual concept, but margin enables spiritual momentum. It gives space for the right kind of attitudes to flourish.

Being Overly Driven

Alongside the concept of margin, some of us are just too driven. My family tends to overwork. My dad is an extremely hard worker, and my brothers and I are the same way. I feel guilty unless I work more than forty hours a week, which means sometimes I cut into playtime or being present with my wife and kids even when I should table my work for the next day. It is great to be a hard worker and to support your family financially, but overworking can be a detriment to our families, our spiritual lives, and our walk with God in the fruit of the Spirit.

If you are overly driven, you may need to pull back the reigns and learn healthier rhythms in life. We are often more irritable and rude when we are trying to get things done at an unhealthy pace. We can't do everything, and we aren't the savior of the world or our workplace. We need to learn to be content doing our part, trust our coworkers, and strive to walk in kindness and gentleness rather than being overly driven.

Aggressiveness

Some people seem kind and gentle on the surface, and then when you least expect it, they bite. Christ doesn't give us a fake sweetness, He gives us a genuine sweetness.

Following Jesus toward kindness and gentleness is not the same as pretending we are okay with everything and lashing out when we can't take it anymore.

We need to be real about our feelings while we walk in kindness. Sometimes, we may need to let go of our strong opinions, and other times, we need to be honest about how we feel and share our feelings in kindness. If we're not careful, our emotions could boil over and lead us to do or say something we will regret.

Call-Out Culture

A handful of Christians love to call people out for their failures. Some identify themselves as discernment bloggers. I've also noticed this call-out culture is prevalent with AM radio preachers and televangelists. Be on guard against call-out culture, where it is prized to speak out against others' failures. This call-out culture is characterized by slander and gossip, but it's sugarcoated by the word *discernment*. Most of what they say tears down or calls out someone else. It is hard to find any fruit of the Spirit that justifies their actions.

The call-out culture seems to believe every "popular" spiritual leader is a wolf in sheep's clothing. Yet those in this culture are constantly seeking attention and popularity. They are some of the least kind people I have ever been in contact with. They claim to be spreading the truth, but they are really just spreading a nasty form of slander masquerading as religion. Beth Moore's daughter Melissa has posted about these types of people, "Nothing strikes me as more contrary to a life of grace than a preoccupation with discovering the worst about other people."[7]

This doesn't mean that a Christian can't call out something unbiblical in a popular preacher's teaching. I just think we need to be far more careful about throwing stones. I am a church leader. I have a Bible college degree. I have read hundreds of Christian books. I've read the Bible cover to cover a dozen times. I've spent my life pursuing the Lord and serving in ministry, yet I would be very, very slow to call out or speak against another Christian. Just because you think someone is wrong, doesn't mean you need to say it out loud or in an ungracious way.

John Maxwell has a powerful framework for discerning who you should accept criticism from. Here are the criteria:

1. They love and care about you.
2. They aren't tainted by a personal agenda.

3. They are not naturally critical of things. (This one has helped me. Just look at a person's past tweets. If they are critical, disregard them.)
4. They are offering genuine support, not just advice.
5. They have legitimate knowledge in the area of their criticism.[8]

Start with the first part: Do they care about you or just their own opinion? Are they genuinely trying to help you or simply trying to get airtime for their own view?

Those are some common challenges to walking in kindness and gentleness. Now let's talk about some practical ways that kindness and gentleness play out in our everyday lives.

Kindness Repents of Past Unkindness

There were times at the beginning of my ministry that I came off too strong. I still wish I could go back to Bible college and have a little more fun and invest more in building friendships. I was too busy and too intense. I'm grateful for the way I grew spiritually during that season of my life, but I wish I would've been more balanced and winsome.

During the summers, I traveled and preached at churches. Being a fresh, young leader, I know I made some mistakes in my zeal. I once preached that we should spend more hours in prayer than we spend watching TV. Afterward, a puzzled young man asked me how he could reasonably attain that spiritual requirement. Another time, although I don't remember saying it, I told my sister-in-law that I was disappointed in how much she watched TV. Years later, when we installed a TV in our bedroom, she was flabbergasted that I would've been so hard on her. I didn't realize then how I came across or how I was recommending spiritual burdens based more in unhealthy intensity than in godly wisdom and kindness. In a very real sense, I was holding people to a spiritual standard instead of focusing on my own heart. I was coming across as unkind, domineering, and dogmatic rather than kind. We need to regularly let the Holy Spirit convict us for unkind words we've said, and unkind attitudes we've let linger in our minds. This is something I always need to remind myself of. As much as I wish I was constantly walking in the fruit of the Spirit, it's all too easy for me to lose my cool and forget to walk in kindness.

I believe some may even weep at the judgement seat of Christ someday for all the careless, harsh, slanderous, and critical words we've spoken about other believers, Christian leaders, and politicians (Matthew 12:36). When we enter the presence of the glorious and merciful God, will we be okay with how we've spoken over the years?

Kindness Listens

My wife and I have a friend who has experienced significant tragedy. As a result, her faith has suffered. She struggles to reconcile how a loving God could allow her to experience so much suffering. When she brings up her doubts, my wife and I respond with care. We offer compassionate encouragement when we can, but most of the time she just needs someone to listen without judging her. Sometimes kindness means listening more than trying to give all the right answers.

Listening well is one of the kindest things you can do.

One of the first steps I would recommend for increasing your kindness is to learn to ask good questions. Learn about others and listen intently, ask follow up questions, and care about their life. Don't do all the talking.

Good conversationalists can share fun personal stories too, but they don't forget to keep the conversation going back and forth. Don't hog the ball. Be generous, and volley it back.

Kindness Gives to People Who Can Never Repay

Kindness looks like this: do favors for people, open the doors of opportunity for others, give without expecting anything in return.

My wife and I have friends like this. They are constantly giving of their time, skills, and resources to help others. Their family business has done incredibly well, and instead of amassing a fortune, they sacrificially give to help more people hear about Jesus. Their example has caused me to grow in my own generosity as a result.

The more we move away from self-interest and begin to give without expecting anything in return, the more we will experience the joy of Christ. I believe that God has hidden joy in His commands. Jesus said, "It is more blessed to give than to receive" (Acts 20:35), and I believe He actually meant it! I've been learning this more in recent years, and I cannot begin to express the joy in my heart as I do.

Not only does God call us to give of our financial resources to the kingdom of God, but He also wants us to give in other areas of our lives: our time, talent, and the totality of our influence. Over the past few years, I have had the privilege of creating opportunities for other young leaders that I would've only dreamed of as a young minister. And as I've helped others, God has given me more and more opportunities to help future leaders.

Do for others what you wished someone would've done for you. Maybe that means mentoring a young parent at church or training an exceptionally sharp young person at your workplace for a role they don't deserve yet. Maybe it means buying your pastor something special. Maybe you can invest in young people who have a passion for the Lord. Find ways to build others up, and give your time, talents, connections, and financial resources.

My friend Casey recently told me, "God's people are some of the most generous people anywhere on earth." This is the people God is calling us to be and the heart He is calling us to have. When we walk in extraordinary generosity, we reveal the kindness of Christ to the people around us.

Kindness Touches Base with People Just Because

Friendship flourishes when you stay in touch. Get together because you care and enjoy the other person's friendship, without an ulterior motive. My lasting friendships are based on selfless and caring actions. We shouldn't check in with people only when we want a favor.

Living a life of kindness means we need to be less self-seeking. It's been said, "God can't fill us with His Holy Spirit if we are already full of ourselves." We need to be careful that we are not selfishly using the people around us but rather loving, serving, and giving to the people God has placed in our lives.

Those Who Know Us Best Respect Us Most

I first met my wife, Michelle, briefly during an outreach in New Orleans. We were both in high school, attending a mostly collegiate mission trip. We really got a chance to spend time together when a mutual friend invited me to attend Michelle's small group. From that first small group I went to, it was love at first sight. I was smitten. (She tells me she was too!) We instantly connected. We couldn't stop talking on the phone and spending time together. After she finished a year-long discipleship program in another state, we immediately began dating. Even the year apart didn't decrease my attraction to her. It was magnetic; irresistible. I couldn't have imagined it was possible to love her more than when we first got married, yet here we are thirteen years later, and our love has only grown deeper. I still learn new things about her. The more I know her, the more I respect and love her. She is the most amazing woman I have ever met. She is full of grace, beauty, humility, authenticity and wisdom. When it comes to her faith, Michelle has always been deeply passionate about the Lord, but in a way that she doesn't need other people to see it or be impressed by it. I've learned about genuine spiritual depth and humility from her more than anyone I've ever met. She is the greatest gift God has given me, and I want to spend the rest of my life loving and cherishing her.

One of the greatest goals we can aim for is that those who know us best respect us the most.

If you're married, you may have noticed that it can be easy to put on a good face for people you hardly see and be unkind toward your spouse or your kids. But what is the kindness and gentleness that Christ calls us to worth if it's not something we practice at home with those who should matter the most to us? The biggest struggle you will have with unkindness will likely take place at home with those closest to you. Keep fighting to walk in kindness at home. Repent to your family when you need to. Apologize and continually work to get better. Never give up trying to show your family how much you love them. They see your imperfections up close, but if you don't give up and keep trying to love them well, they will love you for it.

Let's live in such a way that our kindness is most apparent to those closest to us. Those who know us the best should respect us the most.

Kindness Honors Others

The Bible tells us to "outdo one another in showing honor" (Romans 12:10 ESV). When we honor people around us in practical ways, such as listening to their stories or speaking highly of them and their work, it opens the door for the gospel. Honoring others gives us greater influence with them because they know we care for and respect them.

God wants us to be intentional to honor others, not criticize them. Scriptures that talk about rebuke or judging (those inside the church) are often written to leaders. The Bible clearly says that everyone should honor others. Compete with one another for how much you honor and bless others. What a testament that would be to the kindness of Christ! That would definitely draw new people to the church.

Honor can exhibit our kindness like this:

- Honor teachers and coaches in the community for their investment in young people by giving them gifts to say thank you and scholarships for new equipment.

- Honor police and firemen in the community for their brave service to keep everyone safe by sending a thank you note to the precinct.

- Honor government leaders for their commitment and service to the community. Ask them for ways you can come alongside them to help them, serve the community, and make a difference.

- Honor single moms in the community for their sacrificial effort raising their kids. A church we know gathers volunteers to spend a day fixing cars at no cost for single moms. The church even donates cars to moms in greatest need.

- Honor veterans and their families for their sacrifice and their selfless service to keep our nation safe and free. I know of a ministry that gathers veterans and their families every summer for a getaway to fish and spend time together.

- Honor the leaders of our nation, even when you disagree with them. Don't jump all over every policy issue you disagree with. The Bible tells us to pray for, and show honor to our government leaders, no matter if we agree on everything.

- Honor your pastor's commitment to the Lord and the church. Look for little ways to show your appreciation.

- Honor your parents for raising you, teaching you, and loving you. Respect them and their advice to you. Tell them how much they mean to you, and remind them of specific lessons you learned from them.

- Honor your spouse for their love and commitment to you. Go on dates to talk and celebrate life and love. Take time to emotionally connect. Seek to speak their love language.

Our kindness allows the gospel to be heard and can draw people to faith in Christ.

How Do We Grow in Kindness?

Over the coming week, apply this framework to your words throughout the day: T-H-I-N-K before you speak—is it true, honorable, important, necessary, kind?

Go out of your way to show kindness to your spouse (or a friend or family member if you're single). Give them a thoughtful gift, and tell them how much they mean to you.

Call your parents up. Tell them how much they mean to you and how their sacrifice and love has not gone unnoticed.

Ask God to open your eyes to His kindness throughout the day and to help you be kinder and gentler with everyone you meet.

CHAPTER 6

FAITHFULNESS AND GOODNESS

Make every effort to add to your faith goodness; and to goodness, knowledge; and to knowledge, self-control; and to self-control, perseverance; and to perseverance, godliness; and to godliness, mutual affection; and to mutual affection, love.

2 PETER 1:5–7

The professional networking site LinkedIn reported that recent college graduates in America change jobs four times in the first ten years of their career—twice as often as graduates twenty years ago.[1] As this stat reveals, the idea of faithfulness has changed. While switching jobs is not necessarily always a negative thing, this inability to "stick with things" has translated to other more important areas of our culture like marriage and divorce. People don't know how to stay married anymore, and that affects the very fabric of our culture. We need to relearn what God's Word says about faithfulness and goodness.

Over the past century, we have seen massive shifts in travel, communication, globalization, and literacy. Many of these changes have been for the good of humanity. Even though the human race can split atoms, put mountains of data on a Nano-chip that fits into the palm of your hand, and travel to space, there is still an emptiness and a sinfulness in the human heart. No matter how much advancement we see in science, medicine, and humanitarianism, the problem of the human heart remains. We are lost spiritually without Jesus to save and guide us.

Millennials are the first generation to grow up with the internet widely available. So much has changed, and online accessibility has many positive and negative consequences.

It can be good to take a look back at the generations before us, and consider how they have walked in faithfulness and goodness. I shared earlier about my dad's German Mennonite ancestors, who moved to rural Russia before immigrating to the United States. My grandmother's ancestors were Italian Catholics who were influenced by the Pentecostal movement, and I've heard that they prayed for their future descendants and generations that they would serve the Lord faithfully.

Stories of my wife's relatives and ancestors have had a great influence on me as well. One of those incredible role models for me has been my late grandfather-in-law, G. Mark Denyes. Grandpa Denyes immigrated to the United States from Winnipeg, Canada. He had a pretty good job in banking but got an opportunity in Northern Missouri to be the financial director for a small, private Bible college. So he moved his young family down to Missouri, not knowing exactly what lay ahead. When he arrived in Chillicothe, Missouri, he discovered to his dismay that the finances at the college were in trouble, and the college would have to shut down. And here he had moved his family all this way! He began pastoring at a local church, in addition to working as a traveling cookie salesman. His wife says he was one of the company's best cookie salesmen, but then again, who doesn't want a cookie! By the way, Grandma Denyes still makes some of the best chocolate chip cookies I've ever tasted.

Both Grandpa and Grandma Denyes grew up under difficult circumstances. Grandma Denyes's dad was a car mechanic, who spent his life in a wheelchair. She says he was a sweet man. However, Grandma Denyes's mom struggled with mental health issues that made life challenging for the family. Nevertheless, both Grandpa and Grandma Denyes have turned the tide from their upbringings, established a house full of love, and now have several generations of family members who are loved, prayed for, and taught biblical wisdom. They are a shining example of what the gospel can do in your family.

Grandpa Denyes was born out of wedlock. Before he was born, his mom left town until she had him and gave him up for adoption. His birth parents eventually married, and he had several full siblings, but he didn't meet them for the first time until he was in his late seventies. He had attempted to contact and meet his birth mom later in life, but she didn't want anything to do with him—I don't know the reason. Grandpa Denyes and several of his family members traveled to northern Canada to meet his full-blooded siblings for the first time. It was uncanny how much they all looked, talked, and acted alike, even though they hadn't met until their seventies!

Grandpa Denyes's adoptive parents were Methodist ministers who moved from church to church. His adoptive father, later in his ministry, realized that he had been preaching moralism, not the gospel. He had been telling people to do better and try harder without pointing them to trust Christ alone for salvation. He repented in his journal, broken-hearted at all the souls that he had not guided to the Savior! When we met Grandpa Denyes's birth siblings, mostly a family of teachers and educators, they shared a story about a great relative who had been a Methodist preacher ordained by none other than John Wesley himself!

When we can see the blessings of God over a lifetime, we get a glimpse of the bigger picture that a legacy of faith looks like. If looking back at your ancestors is painful because they did not live well, you can begin a generational legacy. Our actions affect others. Our choice to walk in faithfulness and goodness affects our immediate family, our circle of friends, their families, and generations to come. Walking in faithfulness and goodness can impact so many lives.

I'd like for us to consider how we can walk in faithfulness and goodness.

Our Good Father Is Always Working for Our Good

As a popular worship song says, we have "10,000 reasons" for our hearts to praise God. Whether we notice or not, God is always at work in our lives for our good and His glory. He has an amazing plan for us. God is a good, good Father. He wants what's best for us.

Sometimes life does not seem good because this world is not always good. But there is more goodness than we could ever hope for in God. Pain and hardship are often caused by the devil doing what the devil does: stealing, killing, destroying, and lying to keep people from trusting God. Sometimes pain and hardship are a direct result of our own actions or other people's sinfulness. Proverbs 19:3 says, "People ruin their lives by their own foolishness and then are angry at the LORD" (NLT). Pain in our world doesn't prove God isn't there; pain just proves how much we need to invite God into our world!

The Bible promises us that "God causes everything to work together for the good of those who love God and are called according to his purpose for them" (Romans 8:28 NLT). This means that in all our pain and adversity, God is working for our good. We can trust Him. The Bible goes so far as to say that God's goodness chases us down (see Psalm 23:6; 31:19)!

The Bible tells us that every good thing in your life is a gift from God (James 1:17).

- The latte that you sip as you read this.
- The sensation you get when you watch the sunrise over the mountains.
- The sounds of the ocean roaring against the shore.
- The awe you feel when an epic nature picture of the Faroe Islands crosses your Instagram feed.
- The way your skin breaks to goosebumps when you lightly touch the hand of your spouse.

These are just a few of the many good gifts God gives us. God's goodness is felt by all, by those who choose to serve Him and those who reject Him (Matthew 5:45). How amazing is that?

God reserves even more goodness for those who love Him. Scripture says, "How great is the goodness you have stored up for those who fear you. You lavish it on those who come to you for protection, blessing them before the watching world" (Psalm 31:19 NLT).

God is truly good. He works all things in our life for good.

So why should we strive for faithfulness and goodness? Because our God is faithful and good (1 Corinthians 1:9), and He calls us to follow Him.

God's Word Teaches Us What Is Truly Good

We live at a time when people don't know the difference between good and evil. Several times lately, I have heard people calling evil things good, and good things evil. Recently, I saw one news headline praising a Cuban dictator and his family, and another article blaming the failures of Billy Graham's kids on him being an absentee father. Our generation is illiterate in the teachings of the Word of God, and we suffer for it. God is always speaking into the pain and chaos of our world through His Word, but will we open our Bibles and read?

God's Word teaches us what is good. Ephesians 5:8–10 says, "For you were once darkness, but now you are light in the Lord. Live as children of light (for the fruit of the light consists in all goodness, righteousness and truth) and find out what pleases the Lord." We need to find out what pleases the Lord. This wasn't just written for pastors. No one is exempt. We need to get into the Word of God and commit ourselves to living in a way that pleases Him and understanding what is truly good.

God Has Prepared Good Works for Us to Do

The Bible makes it clear that we are not saved by our good works but only by receiving the gospel. But in the same breath, Paul tells the church in Ephesus, "For we are God's handiwork, created in Christ Jesus to do good works, which God prepared in advance for us to do" (Ephesians 2:10). Not only does God save us by His amazing grace, but He also wants to do so much good through us! God made us for a purpose, and that purpose is directly tied to the idea of loving, serving, and doing good for people around us: our families, our neighborhoods, our work-places, our churches, and our communities.

Not only are we called to walk in good *works*, but we're also called to pursue a deeper goodness. As a fruit of the Spirit, goodness pertains not only to our deeds but also to our motives, our attitudes, and our heart. We are called not simply to serve the homeless at our local soup kitchen but to show them love, joy, kindness, and patience. We are called not simply to serve in our local churches but to encourage and build up the other believers God placed in our lives. We are called not simply to do the dishes after our family meal but to love our family in patience. Goodness encompasses both the good works we do and the heart from which those good works come.

We have covered several big picture considerations. Next, we will look at some more practical examples of walking in faithfulness and goodness.

Be Faithful with the Little Things

"Whoever can be trusted with very little," Jesus taught, "can also be trusted with much" (Luke 16:10). No matter what God has called you to, be faithful in the little things. Do good work in your current position rather than pining for a promotion. Obey the Lord in every area of your life, even the ones that no one sees. He will honor your faithfulness.

My father-in-law, Dwight, has shown me this kind of faithfulness. He was a successful businessman and then stepped into an influential ministry, yet he has shown me how to serve at home. My mother-in-law is an incredible cook, and Dwight decided that when the women cook, the men can clean. He didn't pressure my brother-in-law and me to help him clean, but we quickly followed his example. This small act alone showed me how powerful it can be to serve my wife in small ways.

Keep Your Word

I used to think high spirituality looked or sounded a certain way, but now I know it's more about the little things, our attitudes, and our faithful humility. True spirituality is more about the little things like keeping our word or finishing what we start. Doing every little thing with excellence. Our faithfulness points to and reflects the faithfulness of God to the world.

Character Is Seen When No One Is Watching

It's easy for us to serve the Lord well when people are watching, but your character is seen when no one is watching. Whichever word you use—*character*, *integrity*, or *holiness*—this is a vital part of following Christ and living in goodness and faithfulness.

The book of James says, "We all stumble in many ways" (James 3:2). No one is exempt. In what areas of your life are you quietly struggling to submit to the Lord?

Who we are at home or work when no one is watching reveals whether we are growing in the Lord. Spiritual growth is a very real, lifelong challenge for everyone, even pastors! Oftentimes we can be really good at putting on a spiritual face at church or around strong Christian friends. But we really need to commit our lives to the Lord in the little areas we struggle with when no one is around to motivate us.

If you struggle in your faith or fail in your walk with the Lord, get back up. Never stop repenting and asking God to work in you. "For though the righteous fall seven times, they rise again" (Proverbs 24:16). We rarely notice our own spiritual growth at the time, but over the years, we can see more clearly how God has been at work in us.

Live Your Life for a Higher Purpose

If we live for our own pleasure, wealth, or achievement, we end up wasting our lives.

God has a higher purpose for us. Sometimes following Christ means changing jobs to pursue what He puts on our hearts. More often, it means finding a way to serve in the local church, at a homeless shelter, or in a nonprofit organization. For most of us, following Christ may not mean changing vocations or area codes. However, it might mean searching out a way to use the gifts, roles, and influence we have to serve and honor our King.

What has God called you to? What are your spiritual gifts? Paul taught, "Therefore, my beloved brothers, be steadfast, immovable, always abounding in the work of the Lord, knowing that in the Lord your labor is not in vain" (1 Corinthians 15:58 ESV). God has work for all of us to do, and His Word promises that when we do His work, it makes a real difference both in us and in the world.

It Takes a Lifetime to Give God Our Life

Doing a good deed here and there is great, but God wants more than momentary goodness from us. He wants our whole life. He wants us to live as offerings of praise and thanksgiving to God.

We say that we "give our lives to God," but what does that mean? Since our life is lifelong, it takes a lifetime to fully give away our lives to God. There is no greater privilege than to serve Him for a lifetime.

And here's the deal, God blesses us for our obedience. We will only experience many of God's blessings if we serve Him over a lifetime, not simply for a few years.

I've seen many people lead lifetimes of faithfulness. My late grandpa-in-law and my grandma-in-law, Shirley, are wonderful examples. They have lifetimes of stories of God's faithfulness as they have served Him. It's easy to hear these stories and wish we had our own, but the reality is these stories are hard-earned and can only come from a lifetime of faithfulness.

May Our Good Works Point People to Our Good God

The point of our lives is to point to God. He gave everything for us in Jesus, so let's live wholeheartedly for Him. When you become a Christian, you realize that nothing good comes from you and that everything good comes from Christ. So it would be a travesty if we did good works without pointing people to Him. It's not enough to show people that humanity is full of good people. Whenever you do good, point to the Reason for your goodness.

Pastor Daniel Fusco has said, "I want my life to be a testimony of God's faithfulness. I'll never be perfect, but my life can tell the story of a perfect, faithful God."[2] We do good works and strive to live good and faithful lives for God's glory so that our lives may point to God's goodness. Others should see God's goodness through our lives. Every good thing we do, we owe solely to His grace, which compels us toward faithfulness and goodness for His glory.

So let's walk in faithfulness and goodness, knowing that we will be blessed for it in this life and in eternity. Living to please an audience of One, we live every moment for that day when we will stand before our Lord in heaven and hear the sweet words, "Well done, good and faithful servant! . . . Come and share your master's happiness!" (Matthew 25:21).

How Do We Grow in Faithfulness and Goodness?

Spend time meditating on the goodness and faithfulness of God. He shows us what faithfulness looks like, and we can lean on his goodness and faithfulness. In what ways has he been faithful to you? How can you learn from Him and practice faithfulness?

Do good for someone who needs it. Support a mission trip, give a gift card to someone begging, serve a meal at a local shelter.

How have you failed to keep your word? Apologize to someone if you need to, and recommit to being faithful.

Ask God to teach you His faithfulness and goodness. Ask God to help you grow daily in faithfulness and goodness.

CHAPTER 7

PATIENCE AND SELF-CONTROL

We do not want you to become lazy, but to imitate those who through faith and patience inherit what has been promised.

HEBREWS 6:12

The freshly grilled chicken and bacon settled into my salad, as the avocado and egg blended to the side. Once again, I had the privilege of spending a few hours with one of the wisest people I know, always in the same place in northeast Minneapolis. Every few months we have been getting together at this run-of-the-mill restaurant with extraordinary cobb salads. It's a dream come true for me every time. Some people have dreams of fame, wealth, comfort, or prestige. Most of my dreams involve growing in godly wisdom under a few leaders I admire—to search out and catch godly wisdom from people who have lived with Jesus longer than me. Wisdom is better caught than taught. As the Bible says, "Walk with the wise and become wise" (Proverbs 13:20).

My friendship with Jon Bloom started a few years ago when he messaged me on Twitter. About twenty years ago, Jon Bloom helped John Piper start a ministry called Desiring God. Piper had written a book called *Desiring God*, and it seemed a fitting name for their ministry. Initially, they mailed out cassette tapes of sermons. Their ministry started around the time the internet was taking off. A bivocational New England pastor named Moe enjoyed Piper's sermons. Moe asked if he could begin uploading Piper's sermons online. Twenty years later, much of Desiring God's ministry happens online, and they impact millions of people each day. They have one of the most widely read Christian blogs in the world.

I didn't grow up in Baptist or Reformed circles. I grew up in a Pentecostal evangelical church tradition, but I don't think we need to agree with everything another ministry or denomination believes in order to honor them and glean all the godly wisdom we can from them.

Jon Bloom has become a precious friend. He is full of godly wisdom, and I am truly grateful for the time I get to spend with him. Jon wrote regularly for the *Desiring God* blog, but he didn't start writing his own books until shortly after we met. His first two books, *Not by Sight* and *Things Not Seen*, contain unique discipleship messages, wise biblical insights about what it looks like to live a life of faith even when we don't see how God is working. This working life of faith requires patience and self-control as we trust God to work all things for our good.

I'm an avid reader, and I have been for a long time, but Jon Bloom has quickly become my favorite author. One of the themes of Jon Bloom's writing, and the reason I love it so much, is what it really means to walk by faith. Often, we don't understand how God is working or why He does things differently than we would. Jon wonderfully reminds, provokes, and stirs my soul to trust God even when I don't understand His ways. God's ways truly are higher than our ways. If God's ways line up exactly with our ways, then we should question whether we are actually following God or just ourselves.

In the Christian life, we wait for the world to be made right again, not quite understanding everything God does, and trusting God to help us. This is why we need patience and self-control. No generation has needed patience and self-control more than ours because no generation has had so many options.

It's fascinating how the fruit of the Spirit are shown to work together throughout Scripture. Patience and kindness describe love (1 Corinthians 13:4). The fruit of the Spirit work together in our lives. If you see one fruit, you will often see the others. That is why I'm closing out my discussion on the fruit of the Spirit with patience and self-control. Patience and self-control help us walk in all the other fruit of the Spirit. We need self-control to walk in love rather than anger. We need patience to maintain our joy when we're tempted to get irritated. We need patience and self-control to walk in peace.

The temptation to disregard patience and self-control has only increased through technology. We live in a world of lightning-speed internet. We can get almost anything with the touch of a button. People used to forage or hunt their food and then cook it over a fire they built; now we don't even know where our food comes from. We order our groceries online and have them delivered, or we pick up our food at a drive-through window without ever getting out of our car. Our microwaves, instant coffee, and prepackaged processed food help keep our mealtimes from wasting our precious time. We might as well keep working and checking email while we grab a quick bite. Never has a society been so inexperienced in patience and self-control.

People used to be able to get away from it all, but now FaceTime, messaging, social media, email, and unlimited data keep us constantly plugged in no matter where we go. We go on vacation to a beautiful part of the world and just stare at our phones. You can't even get away from the news anymore—our phones buzz with notifications, our social media is flooded, and our computer screens are invaded with pop-up ads. It's harder than ever to calm down, have patience, or have any semblance of peace when we know virtually every tragedy in every corner the world within minutes. Honestly, it's hard to even process it all in a healthy way, let alone maintain a heart of Christian compassion and mercy.

But even in our constantly connected world, God wants us to learn patience. Our world might move faster now than at any time in history, but that doesn't change God's desire for our patience and self-control. Pastor Mark Batterson has said, "Everything happens at the speed of light. But in God's kingdom, things happen at the speed of a seed planted in the ground that has to take root before it can bear fruit. . . . I can almost guarantee that our hopes and dreams will take longer than our original estimates."[1] God's work in our lives might take a little longer than we expect. The rest of this chapter examines how God does that work in you.

Dallas Willard understood patience and self-control well. John Ortberg writes in his powerful book *Soul Keeping* about his personal friendship with the late Willard. Ortberg describes how he and others experienced a strange phenomenon when they spent time with Willard—their heartbeat would slow down just from being around him. Dallas would tell him, "You must ruthlessly eliminate hurry from your life." Ortberg summarized the lesson he learned from Willard: "For most of us, the great danger is not that we will renounce our faith. It is that we will become so distracted and rushed and preoccupied that we will settle for a mediocre version of it. We will just skim our lives instead of actually living them."[2]

Don't Follow Your Heart, Follow Christ

My generation grew up hearing someone sing, "If it makes you happy, it can't be that bad." Too many of us believe it. We need to consider deeply if our actions will ultimately bring devastating consequences, no matter how happy they make us in the short term.

It is common to hear someone in my generation say, "Follow your heart." The gospel warns against following your heart and tells us instead to follow Jesus. When you commit your life to Christ, and Christ lives in your heart, you have a better chance of your heart telling you the right things. Even so, you always need to line up your decision-making with the Word of God.

One of my pastor friends used to serve as a missionary. During his missionary work, he got caught up in an extramarital affair. He came back to the United States broken and disillusioned. He was the kind of friend you think will never struggle with such blatant sin because of his sterling Christian upbringing. Thankfully, he spent the next several years walking through restoration and counseling. Miraculously his marriage survived, and he and his family have been able to step back into ministry. What kind of advice do you think he needed to hear when his sin was exposed? Did he need to hear, "Follow your heart"? Too often, "Follow your heart" simply means follow your sinful passions. No, my friend knew the only way back to the life he truly desired was to follow Christ.

Self-control is about setting up your future self for success. It's about controlling your present to serve your future. It's a muscle worth training. Don't let your fleeting emotions or sinful passions ruin you. Lead your passions by your will, and let your will be led by God's will.

We are saved by grace through faith in Christ's finished work on the cross. But the Bible clearly calls us to walk daily with self-control and not to give in to sinful passions.

For the grace of God has appeared, bringing salvation for all people, training us to renounce ungodliness and worldly passions, and to live self-controlled, upright, and godly lives in the present age, waiting for our blessed hope, the appearing of the glory of our great God and Savior Jesus Christ, who gave himself for us to redeem us from all lawlessness and to purify for himself a people for his own possession who are zealous for good works. (Titus 2:11–14 ESV)

Be One Step Ahead of Your Struggles

Part of our battle against sin involves being smarter than sin. Don't put yourself in situations where you know you will struggle. Steer clear from the path if you think you won't be able to control yourself.

- If certain TV shows lead you to lust, is it really worth it to try to fast forward and watch the rest of the show? If you simply stopped watching it, wouldn't you be better off?
- If putting yourself in a compromising situation with your boyfriend or girlfriend might lead you to take it too far romantically, why not steer clear of those situations that will only hurt you and your relationship in the end?
- If certain news channels, websites, or emails make you angry and cynical—if they make it difficult for you to control your anger and walk in the fruit of the Spirit— reconsider how much you watch them, or perhaps it is best to turn them off altogether.

The Bible says, "Guard your heart above all else" (Proverbs

4:23 NLT). Paul says to put on spiritual armor (Ephesians 6:10–17). Paul was probably writing about armor while he was under house arrest in Rome. He could simply look across the room or out the door at the soldier who was keeping him from escaping. According to Paul, our heart is covered by the "breastplate of righteousness." You guard your heart by walking righteously, by obeying God's Word, and by self-control, which means saying no to ungodliness and abstaining from "sinful desires which wage war against your soul" (1 Peter 2:11). Sin wars against our souls by drawing us away from God's ways and by blinding us to the divine light of the glory of God in Christ. We have trouble seeing how good God is when we give sin a foothold in our lives.

Is Your Struggle the World, the Flesh, or the Devil? Or Is God Testing You?

Three enemies wage war against our spiritual life on a daily basis: the world, the flesh, and the devil.

The world: Our culture influences us and can pull us away from godliness, patience, and self-control. This might look like the pressure you feel to report extra hours on your time card at work because your coworkers all do it. This could be the temptation to laugh at the crude jokes on Hollywood award shows. The Bible says, "Together they have become corrupt" (Psalm 53:3 ESV). There is a negative influence in our culture that will redirect you away from God. Every morning all over again, you decide who is going to influence you, the world or the Word.

The flesh: Often, the heart of our problem is a problem of our heart. We are pulled away from God by our sinful desires.

We are at fault in what we say because deep down in our hearts we are sinful. And we need to continually submit ourselves to the reign of Christ. The Bible tells us the three big areas where most people struggle: lust, covetousness, and pride (1 John 2:16). Lust happens when we pursue sexual pleasure wrongly. Coveting happens when we want what other people have (or when we struggle with comparison when we scroll through our social media). Pride happens when we think we are better than others, don't need God, or don't need our church. We all need to guard against lust, covetousness, and pride. Of course, there are plenty of other areas of the flesh the Bible warns us about, but these three are the most common. And they're likely the root of our other struggles with our flesh.

The devil: Sometimes our struggles indicate a spiritual attack from the enemy. Typically, Satan tries to steal our joy whenever God does a new work in us or whenever God blesses us. The devil doesn't want us to gain ground for the kingdom of God or to have joy in God. The devil tries to get us to doubt God's goodness and trustworthiness. Maybe the devil wants you to doubt whether God will really bring the right person into your life to marry, and you feel tempted to compromise your values to get someone interested in you. Maybe the devil wants you to doubt whether God is hearing your prayers for a job, and you are tempted to believe you need to make it happen on your own.

Lastly, we might be facing struggles that aren't coming from the world, the flesh, or the devil. The Bible speaks about times when the Lord tests our hearts to see what is in us.[3] It is entirely possible the struggle or waiting season you are going through is from none other than God Himself. God may be testing you to see what is in your heart, to refine you, or to show you how fragile you are without Him. The Bible says that God does this because He loves you and counts you as His children (Hebrews 12:5–11). God takes us just as we are, but He never leaves us just as we are. God sometimes tests us and works in us through our struggles.

One of the Biggest Areas of Struggle Is Our Words

The fruit of the Spirit should be increasingly evident in our thoughts, motivations, actions, and speech. The Bible tells us that our words are one of the most difficult areas to bring under Jesus's reign. We claim to worship God, and yet we speak critically of others.

> We all stumble in many ways. And if anyone does not stumble in what he says, he is a perfect man, able also to bridle his whole body. If we put bits into the mouths of horses so that they obey us, we guide their whole bodies as well. Look at the ships also: though they are so large and are driven by strong winds, they are guided by a very small rudder wherever the will of the pilot directs. So also the tongue is a small member, yet it boasts of great things. How great a forest is set ablaze by such a small fire! (James 3:2–5 ESV)

Do the words coming out of our mouths reflect our sinful flesh or the fruit of the Spirit? Is what you say loving? Is it joyful? Is it peaceful? Is it kind? Is it gentle? Is it good? Is it faithful? Are you speaking out of self-control, or are your words getting the best of you? The words we post online are our words too. Those online posts represent Jesus. We need self-control to filter what we say through the fruit of the Spirit. Truth plus love helps us represent Jesus well to the world, in ways that draw people to the gospel. Our words and attitudes should not be normal—they should seem unusual compared to the way sinful people normally speak.

We Have Different Struggles in Different Seasons

We will have different struggles with patience and self-control in different seasons of our lives. Paul recognized this, and gave Titus specific instructions for encouraging different generations in his congregation:

> Older men are to be sober-minded, dignified, self-controlled, sound in faith, in love, and in steadfastness. Older women likewise are to be reverent in behavior, not slanderers or slaves to much wine. They are to teach what is good, and so train the young women to love their husbands and children, to be self-controlled, pure, working at home, kind, and submissive to their own husbands, that the word of God may not be reviled. (Titus 2:2–5 ESV)

These challenges are still relevant two thousand years later. Let's break them down:

- Are you an older man? Be temperate, self-controlled, sound in faith. Keep running your spiritual race with endurance. But not only be steadfast in your faith, but walk in love for others. Let your life be defined by truth and love. Paul told Timothy, "I want the men everywhere to pray, lifting up holy hands without anger or disputing" (1 Timothy 2:8). Don't let your life be defined by your anger at society and your quickness to start a fight, but by self-control, godliness, prayer, and Christlike love.

- Are you an older woman? Be reverent. Don't spend your time slandering, and don't be addicted to much wine. Older women have much wisdom to teach others. Look for ways to be active in the work of the Lord and to share your wisdom with the next generation.

- Are you a young woman? Love your family well. Be self-controlled. Let your life be defined by purity. Be kind. If you're married, be submissive to your husband. The Bible says, "I also want the women to dress modestly, with decency and propriety, adorning themselves, not with elaborate hairstyles or gold or pearls or expensive clothes, but with good deeds, appropriate for women who profess to worship God" (1 Timothy 2:9–10). This doesn't mean that you can't wear nice things but rather that your priority should be faithful modesty. Let the most attractive thing about you be your walk in the fruit of the Spirit.

- Are you a young man? Be self-controlled. David wrote, "How can a young person stay on the path of purity? By living according to your word" (Psalm 119:9). We need to keep coming back to the Word of God and to grow in self-control, submitting our desires and struggles to God. Proverbs 24:16 tells us, "For though the righteous fall seven times, they rise again." Maybe you need to hear this: keep getting back up. Don't let your struggle have the last word.

Each stage in life requires self-control and patience, in truth and love, to be pleasing to the Lord and influential for the gospel.

God, If You're Not Done Working, I'm Not Done Waiting

So much of life, even the Christian life, is spent in God's "waiting room"—waiting on Him to work, help, and empower us. We are not in control of our lives, even though sometimes we act like we are. Our seasons of rest and waiting point us to God's sovereignty. He is in control of our life and world, not us.

If you are waiting on God for something, remember how He has been faithful to you in the past, and remind yourself of all He has done for you in the gospel. Know that if He wants you to wait, there has to be a good reason. Faith is trusting God more than we trust ourselves.

Our generation also needs to learn to press God when we don't see an answer. We need to learn to stay active as we wait on God and keep praying until we get a clear answer. Sometimes this means we keep on praying for years. The wait will be worth it in the end if we do not give up on praying in faith.

Maybe you are waiting for the right relationship in your life. You see others finding good relationships, and you wonder when it will be your turn. Don't search for a shortcut out of the season God has you in. Don't date just because you can't sit still. Don't date out of fear you won't find someone. Trust that God cares about this area of your life, and He will lead you to the right person at the right time. Focus on Him in this season, and becoming the person you need to be for the relationship you are praying for.

There Are Spiritual Benefits to Waiting

You might be waiting on God for something. Maybe you're waiting on an answer to a prayer request you've been bringing to God for years. Maybe you're waiting for comfort or relief after loss or hardship. Maybe you're waiting on God for greater opportunity to serve His kingdom. God is working in us as we wait on Him. The only path to spiritual maturity goes through struggles and seasons of waiting.

There is a spiritual maturity that only comes from seasons of waiting. "Consider it pure joy, my brothers and sisters, whenever you face trials of many kinds, because you know that the testing of your faith produces perseverance. Let perseverance finish its work so that you may be mature and complete, not lacking anything" (James 1:2–4).

Seasons of waiting are stepping stones on our faith journeys that lead us toward making a difference in the world. Seasons of waiting are part of an active and effective Christian life.

> For this very reason, make every effort to add to your faith goodness; and to goodness, knowledge; and to knowledge, self-control; and to self-control, perseverance; and to perseverance, godliness; and to godliness, mutual affection; and to mutual affection, love. For if you possess these qualities in increasing measure, they will keep you from being ineffective and unproductive in your knowledge of our Lord Jesus Christ. (2 Peter 1:5–8)

When we go through adversity with patience and self-control, we find favor with God: "For this finds favor, if for the sake of conscience toward God a person bears up under sorrows when suffering unjustly. For what credit is there if, when you sin and are harshly treated, you endure it with patience? But if when you do what is right and suffer for it you patiently endure it, this finds favor with God" (1 Peter 2:19–20 NASB). Sometimes when we pray, God delivers us from pain or hardship, and sometimes we are called to "endure suffering . . . as a good soldier of Christ Jesus" (2 Timothy 2:3 NLT). We cannot simply pray all of life's difficulties away by working up enough faith. That is not how following Christ works. God in His Word repeatedly calls us to live in patient endurance, and He wants to do a good work in us during these seasons of waiting. We probably didn't choose to be in a waiting season, but God is working in you when you are waiting on Him.

The promises of God are not simply inherited by having enough faith. They are inherited by faith and patience. Trust that God will do what He promised. The writer of Hebrews says, "We do not want you to become lazy, but to imitate those who through faith and patience inherit what has been promised" (Hebrews 6:12). Hebrews challenges us not to be lazy as we wait patiently.

God calls us to active waiting. We should get busy serving our local church, community, and anyone who needs our help. We should love the people God placed in our lives. We should walk in the fruit of the Spirit and make every effort to please God for all His grace in our lives. We might feel like God surely has more important things for us to do. But no matter what season we are in, we can always walk in a way that is pleasing to the Lord and shines God's grace on the world around us.

God Is at Work in the Interruptions of Your Life

We don't know what tomorrow holds. That is one of the great undergirding principles of our spiritual lives. God doesn't often show you the next ten steps of your life all at once. He periodically shows you things that are far off, the dreams and plans He has for you, but usually He shows you simply what He wants next for you.

For some people, you are not quite sure where God is leading you, and that's okay too. Keep seeking, asking, and knocking in prayer for God's guidance in your life.

Be obedient in the little things. We can't expect God to answer the big questions, when we are unfaithful in the small things in our daily life.

Even when we have a sense of God's leading in our lives, life often turns out differently than we expect or hope. But when we look back over the years, we can see how God has been leading and preparing us. Praise God for those moments when we look back and see the beautiful way He has woven together our stories.

A lot of Jesus's ministry was due to interruptions. People came to him for miracles while He was in the middle of doing something else. God specializes in working in the interruptions of our lives and wants us to remain flexible in the plans and purposes He has for us.

Among the interruptions of life, we must prioritize people over projects and loving others over accomplishing tasks. God cares more about the people we are becoming than about what we are accomplishing.

Keep in Step with the Spirit

Self-control and patience are all about keeping in step with the Spirit.

Some Christian denominations talk a lot about being filled with the Holy Spirit. I grew up in a denomination like that. Being filled with the Holy Spirit is an important biblical truth that every Christian would do well to consider and seek. But we also need to talk about what it means to keep in step with the Spirit, following the Spirit's lead, living in the fruit of the Spirit, and walking in love, joy, peace, patience, kindness, gentleness, faithfulness, goodness, and self-control. A one-time event of being filled with the Spirit can be life-changing, but we also need fresh reminders and experiences of God's Spirit.

The Spirit empowers us toward greater self-control, patience, and love (2 Timothy 1:7). Self-control and patience help us walk in the other fruit of the Spirit. Self-control and patience keep us in step with the Spirit. They are the habit of continually submitting our thoughts, motivations, actions, words, and online posts to the Lord as we represent Him to the world.

How Do We Grow in Patience and Self-Control?

Watch for times when you struggle with patience and begin to make those areas a matter of prayer for change.

While driving this week, when you may normally get angry at a car in front of you, instead check yourself, and pray God's blessing on them. Share this commitment with a friend or family member who can hold you accountable.

Give yourself ten extra minutes to get to work every day this week. See how it affects your attitude.

Put your work down thirty minutes early and get home earlier than usual. See how your family responds. If you are single, how can you set aside work, and spend meaningful time with the people who matter most to you?

If you're in a waiting season, consider how you can participate in active waiting by serving God and your church even when you don't know what's next.

Ask God to astonish you with His patience in the Scriptures. Ask God to help you exhibit patience and self-control.

CHAPTER 8

TRUTH

For God so loved the world that he gave his one and only Son, that whoever believes in him shall not perish but have eternal life.

JOHN 3:16

Billy Graham passed away in early 2018 nearly one hundred years after he was born. That day, America—and the world, really— lost one of the greatest evangelists of all time. He undoubtedly communicated the gospel message to more people face-to-face than anyone in human history. Three hundred million people heard him share the simple gospel message live, and countless millions more watched and listened through television, radio broadcasts, and online videos. I am among those who got to hear Billy Graham preach the gospel live. As a boy, I attended his 1996 Minneapolis Crusade. I remember DC Talk rocking out the Metrodome and then hearing Billy Graham share the gospel. I remember being astonished as thousands of people from all over the stadium made their way down to the front of the stage, with tears running down their cheeks, to make a decision of faith in Jesus Christ.

We lost a living legend. In a biography written in the 1960s, the author called a prominent Christian preacher the "Billy Graham of South Africa." People have been using variations of that phrase for nearly sixty years! Phrases like that point to the way God used Billy Graham, who maintained his humility, integrity, and focus on the gospel. Billy Graham's message was "Christ is the only answer to the deepest needs of the human heart."

While sharing my thoughts online after his death, I was invited as a guest to reminisce about Billy Graham's legacy with

BBC World News Service alongside several other guests throughout the day. The first several questions were about what it was like
to hear Billy Graham live and to discuss how expansive his impact
was. The final question mentioned a controversial statement Billy
had made many years ago and asked us to respond. They said,
"People say Billy Graham was intolerant. What do you think?" I
was caught off guard. But I expressed my belief that anyone can
throw out opinions online nowadays without knowing someone.
For everyone who knew Billy Graham or was acquainted with
him, he was incredibly loving and gracious.

A few weeks later, as I was reading Billy Graham's autobiography *Just as I Am*, I realized how many times the press around
the world had asked him similar questions. Before Billy Graham's
first London crusade, he faced a flurry of angry media criticism
and questions. Ironically, all the negative media attention gave
the crusade much more press and public interest than it ever
would have had without the criticism. Years later, when Billy
Graham was back in England, the press had become friendlier
after seeing the ways God had used him positively in the region.
During that visit, he had the opportunity to meet C. S. Lewis,
who wasn't yet widely known in America for *The Chronicles of
Narnia* or *Mere Christianity*. Billy's wife, Ruth, had been reading
The Chronicles of Narnia prior to the trip. C. S. Lewis greeted
Billy Graham as they spent some time together, and said, "You
have many critics Billy Graham, but no one who has actually
met you has a single bad thing to say about you."[1]

In our world, it is easier than ever to make divisive, critical,
and blanket statements about others. We think we can say whatever we want without spiritual consequences. But the Bible calls
us to a different way of speaking and living.

Why would anyone think Billy Graham was intolerant? In part, it is because Billy Graham would preach the Bible, preach against sin, and call people to Christ as the only answer to lasting peace and joy in the human heart. People think he was intolerant in part because he believed what the Bible has to say about human sinfulness.

Society is changing these days. The *New Yorker* recently posted an article about "Chick-fil-A's Creepy Infiltration of New York City." The article says, "The brand's arrival here feels like an infiltration, in no small part because of its pervasive Christian traditionalism."[2] Seriously? The people touting tolerance in our culture have become surprisingly intolerant about Christians. If the *New Yorker* article had been about a restaurant with owners from any other religious group, it would never have been allowed to be published, not even by the *National Enquirer*. People are okay with intolerance toward people they think are intolerant. Jesus taught, "You will be hated by everyone because of me, but the one who stands firm to the end will be saved" (Matthew 10:22). And "This is the verdict: Light has come into the world, but people loved darkness instead of light because their deeds were evil" (John 3:19).

Truth is not always popular. Sometimes the truth gets you in trouble. But God calls us to walk in both His love and His truth, no matter the consequences.

Billy Graham has written about a season where he wrestled with the truth of God's Word.[3] He had been traveling around the United States and the United Kingdom doing large youth rallies for an organization called Youth for Christ. One of the other speakers, Chuck Templeton, was on some of those trips with him, and they became good friends. Chuck had begun seminary and had started to wrestle with the authority of God's Word. He had come to believe there were errors in the Bible that couldn't be resolved and that the Bible was antiquated in parts. Chuck, even as a pastor, began to believe the Bible couldn't be taken literally, and he asked his friend Billy some of his questions. One time, the two men had both traveled to the San Bernardino Mountains in Southern California to speak at a camp called Forest Home run by a Christian educator named Henrietta Mears. Billy, still wrestling with Chuck's questions, told Henrietta what he was going through, and that he felt too weary to fulfill his speaking engagement. Henrietta, along with another leader, J. Edwin Orr, gave Billy some incredible insights about the authority of God's Word—good answers to the questions Chuck was raising. For example, Jesus spoke regularly about the Old Testament stories as truth. So if we can trust Jesus, we can trust the Bible.

That evening, Billy made his way down a mountain trail near the camp and laid his Bible on a tree stump. He cried out to God in prayer: "God I don't understand everything about your Word, or have answers to all the questions that Chuck is raising, but I put my trust in Your Word, by faith." Tears stung his cheeks, and he sensed the presence of God overwhelm him in a way he hadn't felt for many months. The next morning, Billy fulfilled his obligation to preach at Forest Home. He preached with a new authority, and hundreds of people made decisions for Jesus Christ at the service. Just a few weeks later, Billy Graham began preaching a planned series of meetings, which became his historic 1949 LA crusade. The crusade was picked up by major media outlets and ultimately thrust his ministry into the national spotlight. Many celebrities (including Louis Zamperini), media personalities, and even mobsters made decisions for Jesus Christ throughout this crusade.

Interestingly, Chuck Templeton, who had asked Billy the questions, eventually denounced his Christian faith and went on to become a well-known broadcaster in Canada. My friend Lee Strobel had an opportunity to meet with Chuck late in his life at his penthouse suite in Toronto. During the day they spent together, Lee asked him about his struggle and search for truth throughout his life. As a former atheist, Lee tried to give Chuck good answers he had discovered along his own spiritual journey. At one point, Chuck confessed to Lee, "I miss Jesus." After spending most of his life denying the truth of Jesus, Chuck couldn't get away from the longing in his heart for Jesus.

In a day when people feel like they can believe whatever they want, and no one is allowed to tell them otherwise, we need truth plus love more than ever.

We Can Know Truth through Our Bibles

I shared a quote on Twitter a few years ago, and it went viral: "Don't say God is silent when your Bible is closed." I'm not sure where the quote comes from, but it resonated with people. These ten words rebuke our fear that God might be inactive or uncaring in the brokenness and messiness of our lives. The quote reminds us that He cares, He sees, and He speaks. But too often, we're just not listening. God is active and speaking into the chaos of our lives and of our world, but will we open our Bibles and listen to Him? When we open the Bible, we find more than 750,000 words breathed out by God himself for us.

Charles Spurgeon said, "Nobody ever outgrows Scripture;

the Book widens and deepens with our years."[4] In my thirty-five years on this earth, I have consistently experienced the Bible's ability to speak the right word at the right time. My late grandfather-in-law, who spent his life as a pastor, testified to the same: God's Word continued to be fresh and continued to speak in new ways even though he'd read the same words countless times.

The Bible is the most amazing book in all of history. The history of how God's Word has come to us today is an astonishing story:

- The Scriptures have proven their historical accuracy with each new archeological discovery. Much reasonable evidence is available to trust the accuracy of the Scriptures.
- Many who have worked to bring the Scriptures to new people groups and in new languages have done so at great personal cost. Their sacrifice speaks volumes about its reliability.
- The Scriptures have influenced people in positive ways throughout history. The Bible has rescued, recreated, and mobilized billions.
- Some have misused the Bible to do horrible things, and we should lament and repent of this. But many more have been mobilized to do good. If we submit ourselves to Scripture as God's living Word, we can trust it to shape our world in ways only God can bring about.

God wants to give us countless blessings and wisdom that can only come through the truth of His Word. We can know truth that will change our lives for the better when we open our Bibles.

If We Move Away from the Truth of God's Word, We Move Away from the Power to Save

I have come to the firm belief that the truth of Jesus is where the power is! Romans 1:16 says, "For I am not ashamed of the gospel, because it is the power of God that brings salvation to everyone who believes: first to the Jew, then to the Gentile." We only hurt ourselves when we move away from the grace, freedom, joy, peace, and hope that God wants to fill us with!

Augustine is often quoted as saying, "If you believe what you like in the Gospel, and reject what you don't like, it is not the Gospel you believe, but yourself." There is a danger in becoming a rule unto ourselves. We decide that we know better than God, or we can at least help Him along the way. We remove the parts of the Bible that we like and leave out the rest—to our detriment. I am thankful that God knows more, understands deeper, and loves so much greater than my puny ability, or yours.

There are core truths in the gospel that we must believe in order to walk in the truth of Jesus:

- We are all sinful and need a Savior. We can't save ourselves. Our sin harms our lives and the lives of others. Even knowing this, we still continue to sin. We need Christ to save us from ourselves.
- Many people agree that Jesus is the greatest teacher ever. But Jesus called Himself the only way to God. He came and lived a sinless life and died on a brutal cross. He shed His blood to take our sins on Himself and redeem us. He rose again on the third day and sits at the right hand of the Father in heaven to receive those who come to Him.

- We are saved by God's grace through faith in Jesus. It is not enough to simply go to church, or even read the Bible and pray. We need to believe in and receive Jesus and follow Him.

- We are called to repent—to turn from our sin, and to follow Jesus. Our struggle with sin is a lifelong battle, but we are called to make every effort to turn from sin and follow Jesus. Often, people who turn to Jesus experience a dramatic change in their thoughts, attitudes, words, and lifestyle. My friend Lee Strobel was an atheist before coming to believe in the truth of Christ. While he loved his family, he often found himself hurting them by his drinking, his temper, and his rudeness. His marriage was on the rocks, and when he came to Christ it changed everything. Thanks to the work of Jesus in his life, and repentance, he and Leslie just celebrated their forty-six-year anniversary. They would be the first to say they aren't perfect. And they'd also say that choosing to follow Jesus instead of themselves made an incalculable difference in their lives.

- We are sinful, disobedient to God, and deserve hell, which was prepared for the devil and his angels. The worst part about hell is eternal separation from God. Those who reject God don't realize how terrible separation will be, but they still choose it. But if we believe in and receive Christ, we are brought from death to life and will spend eternity in heaven with God after we die!

In our generation, entire major denominations have been moving away from the truth of God's Word and allowing sinful lifestyles to remain unchecked. They even let pastors live in openly sinful lifestyles and expect the power of God to remain in their churches. God doesn't bless a church that moves away from the truth of His Word. They are unplugging the power cord. It's no wonder that these denominations are losing adherents by the thousands every year. When denominations move away from the truth of God's Word, they lose the power to save.

Those who say that Christians can live comfortably in sin are walking away from the truth of Jesus. The writer of Jude wrote about this, "For certain individuals whose condemnation was written about long ago have secretly slipped in among you. They are ungodly people, who pervert the grace of our God into a license for immorality" (Jude 4).

If we claim to walk in love but leave truth behind, we are only extending counterfeit love, and we are losing the power of God to save and transform people. The power to love others resides in passing the truth of God's Word to others, not editing the message to fit our liking.

Truth Is Given to Build Others Up, Not Tear Them Down

The Bible tells us about the truth of God's Word, which "is alive and active. Sharper than any double-edged sword, it penetrates even to dividing soul and spirit, joints and marrow; it judges the thoughts and attitudes of the heart" (Hebrews 4:12). The truth of God's Word can be sharp. The Bible compares itself to a double-edged sword. But this sword is more like a surgeon's scalpel for spiritual surgery. Rebecca Manley Pippert states, "God's wrath is not a cranky explosion, but his settled opposition to the cancer of sin which is eating out the insides of the human race he loves with his whole being."[5] God wants to perform spiritual surgery in our lives through His Word. God wants to remove what harms and destroys us. God's Word only cuts us in order to heal us and build us up.

Christine Caine has said, "God didn't come to say shame on you, but to say shame off you."[6] God only shames the enemy of our souls: "In this way, he disarmed the spiritual rulers and authorities. He shamed them publicly by his victory over them on the cross" (Colossians 2:15 NLT). Have you been living with shame or felt ashamed before God? He wants to take that from you and nail it to the cross. He wants you to be overwhelmed by His love, not by your shame.

When Paul talked about the authority God had given him, he noted that it was authority to build people up, not to tear them down (2 Corinthians 13:10). God wants us to be agents of His healing work in the world, not add to the division, criticism, hate, shame, and brokenness in our world. We wield powerful words of truth, but we need to wield them responsibly, to build people up, not tear them down (Proverbs 16:21).

Truth Hurts Because It Exposes Our Sinfulness and Self-Dependency

The truth of the gospel tells us how sinful we are, which is one of the main reasons people don't want to believe. We think we're not that bad, or at least that our good deeds outweigh our bad. But the gospel exposes that we are so sinful we needed God to die in our place.

The Bible says we can't see the truth because we don't want to see it. "In their own eyes they flatter themselves too much to detect or hate their sin" (Psalm 36:2). Some people mock the idea of repentance or turning from their sin. They ignore or suppress their guilty consciences. But godly people acknowledge their sin and seek to live a life of repentance. (Proverbs 14:9) When we read the Bible, it exposes our flattering view of ourselves. We are spiritually sick. We are sinful. We are wrong. We can't save ourselves. We need a Savior.

Pastor Choco De Jesus has stated, "In a culture of tolerance, repentance has become a dirty word. But without repentance we can't experience cleansing, refreshing, and renewal."[7]

Truth Removes What Hinders Love

My mom once shared her faith with a lady outside a grocery store. As they were putting their groceries into their neighboring cars, my mom told the woman, "Jesus loves you." The woman said, "Thank you so much. So many people have told me that lately." My mom felt called to respond, "Jesus wants you to love him back." That seven-word sentence changed the trajectory of that woman's life forever. She started attending our church, was overwhelmed by the love and support she felt there, and was soon set free from decades of abuse and sinful habits. She now travels and speaks and writes about the freedom she found in the truth of Jesus. But she had to be confronted with truth. Jesus loves you, but are you loving Him back?

The love chapter in Corinthians tell us that "love does not delight in evil but rejoices with the truth" (1 Corinthians 13:6). Just as love and kindness and patience and the other fruit of the Spirit are inseparable from each other, so truth is connected to love.

Walking in the truth of Jesus is simply loving God in all the ways He first loved us. Billy Graham has said,

> This generation finds it difficult to believe that God hates sin. I tell you that God hates sin just as a father hates a rattlesnake that threatens the safety and life of his child. God loathes evil and diabolic forces that would pull people down to a godless eternity just as a mother hates a venomous spider that is found playing on the soft, warm flesh of her little baby. It is His love for man, His compassion for the human race that prompts God to hate sin with such a vengeance.[8]

What a perspective changer! God's truth keeps us away from sin for a very good reason: sin keeps us from life, real love, lasting joy, peace, and wholeness. Sin keeps us from God, where we find all those things in abundant measure.

Truth Sets Us Free

Jesus said, "If you hold to my teaching, you are really my disciples. Then you will know the truth, and the truth will set you free" (John 8:31–32). The truth of Jesus is not some bondage to keep you from the life you want to live. The truth of Jesus sets you free. It's liberating! Likewise, Paul told Timothy about the freedom that can be experienced in Jesus, "He gave his life to purchase freedom for everyone. This is the message God gave to the world at just the right time" (1 Timothy 2:6 NLT).

Living in truth means walking in freedom you wouldn't otherwise know. "It is for freedom that Christ has set us free. Stand firm, then, and do not let yourselves be burdened again by a yoke of slavery" (Galatians 5:1). "Through Christ Jesus the law of the Spirit who gives life has set you free from the law of sin and death" (Romans 8:2). The freedom we have because of the gospel is freedom from crushing religious rules, the enslavement of sin, and the fear of death.

While religion says *do*, Jesus says *done*. That is the truth of the gospel. On the cross, Jesus said, "It is finished." Our religious rules and human attempts couldn't get us to God. Once and for all, Jesus paid the price for us to come to God. The gospel says it's no longer about the good things I do but about the goodness imparted to me through Christ. Yes, Jesus saved us in order to follow Him, but we are saved solely by what He has done, not by anything we can do. We are needy for the gospel every day. Relying on Christ and the gospel brings incredible freedom and actually motivates us to follow Him with joy and peace rather than guilt or religious duty.

John wrote, "My dear children, I write this to you so that you will not sin. But if anybody does sin, we have an advocate with the Father—Jesus Christ, the Righteous One" (1 John 2:1). We should make every effort to walk in holiness, but when we do sin, we will always come back to Jesus's work, not our own.

Jesus doesn't save you so you can keep on sinning. He saves you so you can follow Him. Jesus doesn't offer us freedom *to* sin but freedom *from* sin. The freedom He gives us is that He draws us away from the sin that enslaves us. No longer do our sinful habits have the power to trap and destroy us.

One gentleman who attends our church has been set free from a life of drug and alcohol addiction. Before he came to faith in Jesus, he hurt countless people, including his kids and family. After Christ freed him from sin, he became a gentle giant and a "man's man" full of truth and love. He is still working to restore the broken relationships from his past, but he enjoys overwhelming peace, joy, and love through his freedom in the truth of Jesus.

We may always struggle with sin, but when we embrace the truth of Jesus, we can rely on His victory. When we trust in Jesus, He has already set us free. We will experience His freedom fully in heaven.

When you embrace the truth of Jesus, not only does your heart explode with love, joy, and peace, but you feel the freedom that only He can give!

Truth Brings Us Closer to God

Truth brings us into the lasting happiness and satisfaction of relationship with God. In no other place can we find satisfaction that will last. When we draw close to God, we find all the satisfaction and peace our heart has been longing for. God created us for Himself, and as Augustine famously said, our hearts are restless until they rest in Him.[9]

Truth Is a Person

Other religions promote good works. Some religions even seem to outdo Christians in how disciplined they are. What makes Christianity different or more truthful than the rest of the religions in the world? Christ alone is the difference. We don't follow a religious system; we follow Jesus.

In other words, the truth is not merely some theory or concept. The truth is a *person*.

While other religions reach out to God, Christianity shows the truth of God reaching out to us in Jesus. God reaches down with profound love, kindness, and grace to bring us to Him.

The Bible says about the truth of Jesus:

For it is my Father's will that all who see his Son and believe in him should have eternal life. (John 6:40 NLT)

Yet to all who did receive him, to those who believed in his name, he gave the right to become children of God. (John 1:12)

Billy Graham shared a powerful story in his autobiography about the longing in all of our hearts for the truth of Jesus. He and Ruth were spending time on an island in the Caribbean:

One of the wealthiest men in the world asked us to come to his lavish home for lunch. He was seventy-five years old, and throughout the entire meal he seemed close to tears. "I am the most miserable man in the world," he said. "Out there is my yacht. I can go anywhere I want to. I have my private plane, my helicopters. I have everything I want to make me happy. And yet I'm as miserable as hell." We talked with him and had prayer with him, trying to point him to Christ, who alone gives lasting meaning to life.

Then we went down the hill to the small cottage where we were staying. That afternoon the pastor of the local Baptist church came to call. He was an Englishman, and he too, was seventy-five. A widower, he spent most of his free time taking care of his two invalid sisters. He reminded me of a cricket—always jumping up and down, full of enthusiasm and love for Christ and for others. "I don't have two pounds to my name," he said with a smile, "but I'm the happiest man on this island."

"Who do you think is the richer man?" I asked Ruth after he left.

We both knew the answer.[10]

What does it profit us if we gain the whole world, and yet lose our soul? What does true success look like? What is life all about? The answer is found in a person, Jesus, who calls us to walk in both truth and love.

Have you received God's love for you in the truth of Jesus? The Son of God came as man, lived a sinless life, died on the cross, and rose again on the third day. He now sits at the right hand of the Father and will receive all those who trust in Him to heaven one day.

Going to church doesn't make you a Christian any more than going into Burger King makes you a Whopper. Being near church and other Christians isn't enough. What matters is reaching out to Jesus with faith and receiving Him into your life. What matters is the eighteen-inch journey from your head to your heart.

Yes, Jesus loves you, but will you receive His love for you by believing in the truth of Jesus? When we believe in the truth of Jesus, we experience the love of God that we've heard about, and God's love will change everything in our lives if we let it.

If that is you, this is your moment—don't turn another page, until you bow your head in prayer. Today, put your trust in Jesus and what He has done for you, and experience God's amazing love!

How Do We Grow in Truth?

Over the coming week, start a one-year Bible reading plan. Commit a few minutes each morning or evening to read God's Word. Each time as you begin reading, ask God to open your eyes to His truth. As you finish reading, consider one thing you read that you can begin to apply in your life.

Have you ever used truth to hurt someone else? Even someone online? Consider going back to that post and deleting it or apologizing to the person you offended.

Pray and ask God to help you fall in love with His truth.

If you prayed to trust in Jesus at the end of this chapter, we would love to hear from you. Send us your contact information at thinke.org/gospel. We want to send you some powerful resources about growing in your faith in Jesus.

CHAPTER 9

UNCOMMON INFLUENCE

Speaking the truth in love, we will grow to become in every respect the mature body of him who is the head, that is, Christ.

EPHESIANS 4:15

Tears filled Henrietta's eyes as she and her sister surveyed the destroyed buildings and poverty-stricken people across Europe after the war ended and Nazi Germany was overthrown.[1] She and her sister had been on a year-long sabbatical from the church. They had been spending time in South America, but Henrietta couldn't shake the desire to see the devastation from World War II firsthand. She was able to pull some strings to get a visa. She told the officials, "Over 700 young men from our church fought in Europe, and I want to see for myself what conditions prevail there, so I can better counsel them when I return home."[2]

Henrietta Mears and her sister were able to secure visas, and they made the voyage by ship to France. Everyone they met had been affected by the war. One night at dinner, she learned that her dining companion's entire family had been killed during the war. They traveled through Rome, Brussels, Paris, and Berlin and wept at the destruction, death, and poverty left in the wake of the war. She wrote in her journal about the destruction she saw. Her heart was broken. She felt an increased urgency to reach the world with the gospel.

Henrietta returned home to America and to her role as Christian education director at Hollywood Presbyterian Church with a renewed burden and vision. She saw clearly, while in Europe, the direction that humanity would go without the truth of Jesus. She began to teach and minister with a new urgency for the world to know the truth of Jesus.

A few months later, on Tuesday night, June 24, 1947, during the college leadership retreat at the Christian camp she founded, Forest Home, in the San Bernardino mountains, she spoke about what she had experienced in Europe. She began to tell them about a term she had heard from the war: *expendables.* She told them there must be a Christian answer to the problems the world is facing. "God has an answer. Jesus said we must make disciples of all men. We are to take His gospel to the ends of the earth. God is looking for men and women of total commitment. During the war, men of special courage were called upon for difficult assignments; often these volunteers did not return. They were called 'expendables.' We must be expendables for Christ."[3]

God's presence filled the room as she taught. There was a vivid sense of greater things God was doing, and about to do through this group. Four young men were especially moved as she preached. After her message that night, they followed her and asked to pray. They knelt together and began to pray into the late hours of the night. There was much weeping, crying out to the Lord. During the night, God gave them a vision of college campuses of the world being reached with the gospel, and activated to change the world for Christ. In that group of four young men, were:

- Richard Halverson, who spent decades as the US Senate Chaplain
- Louis Evans Jr., who became the pastor of National Presbyterian Church, where most American presidents have attended and Queen Elizabeth and Mother Teresa have visited
- Jack Franck, who went on to lead Hollywood Presbyterian Church

- Bill Bright, who later founded Campus Crusade for Christ

They sensed they should quickly pull together a college conference for leaders and students around the country. They used another war term, calling it the "College Briefing Conference" to indicate the seriousness of the task to reach the world with the truth of Jesus. There was a sense about their efforts as they reached out to leaders around the nation. Hundreds gathered two months later, and the presence of God was breaking out in definite revival. This move of God continued into following years of the College Briefing Conference, and as students traveled and ministered in other places sharing what God was doing.

As I mentioned earlier, two years later Billy Graham came to speak at Forest Home. A few weeks after, the historic LA crusade took place. In fact, it was Henrietta inviting Billy to speak to her "Hollywood Christian Group" that led to many celebrities and media personalities coming to faith in Christ at the crusade, which in turn led to much of the media attention that followed.

Henrietta's efforts led to many spiritual movements and prompted many young people to carry the truth of Jesus to millions around the world over the coming decades. In addition to Billy Graham and the four others mentioned above, Henrietta discipled the founder of the Navigators, the founder of Young Life, the chairman of World Vision, and even President Ronald Reagan, among many others. Near the end of her life, a special get together was held at her home with many of her students, who were now in ministry and leading influential organizations. She made a list and discovered that more than fifty influential Christian organizations had been started by her students.

.

Henrietta lived her life full steam ahead in truth plus love. She dedicated her life to studying and sharing the truth of Jesus. She loved God's Word and knew its power to change lives. The fruit of the Spirit enabled her effective and influential ministry for the Lord. Before she moved to Hollywood, she was a teacher in the Minneapolis public school system, but in midlife, she was invited to lead the Christian education department at Hollywood Presbyterian Church. During the second half of her life there, their youth ministries grew in weekly attendance from hundreds to more than six thousand. Her pastor said of her, "Perhaps the greatest impact our church has had over the years, has been the ministry of Henrietta Mears."[4]

Even toward the end of her life, Henrietta longed to grow closer to the Lord. People who knew her said of this time of seeking the Lord, that after, "she was even more sympathetic, gracious, kind and secure."[5] She is a brilliant example of what God can do with someone who walks in both truth plus love.

The fruit of the Spirit are not simply cardboard cutouts we learned about in Sunday School. They are powerful traits that can transform every aspect of our lives. God doesn't just want to save our soul. He wants to set us wholly on the path of godly wisdom. This is why each aspect of the fruit of the Spirit is essential.

When we walk in the truth and love of God, God can use us at max capacity for His purposes. It's difficult to overestimate what God can do through someone who has both truth and love. Do you remember the formula I shared at the beginning of this book? Truth plus love equals influence. I believe that walking in truth plus love gives us greater influence.

- We will have greater influence at home with our families

as we serve them and live in integrity, graciousness, love, and purpose.

- We will have greater influence at our workplaces if we serve those we work with and treat others with dignity, kindness, and respect. We should listen to our coworkers more than we talk, care about their lives, and do our work assignment as if working for the Lord, not men.
- We will have greater influence in our neighborhoods as we practice self-control in our responses toward others and exhibit a joyful, peaceful attitude in our conversations and interactions.
- We will have greater influence in our communities as we seek the peace of our city and pray for our government leaders and those in authority.
- We collectively will have greater influence in our nation as Christians resound both truth and love and our inter-actions show a different way forward than what culture offers. Instead of divisiveness, criticism, cynicism, hate, cursing, we offer love to those who hate us, grace to the ungracious, peace to the frantically fearful.
- We will have greater influence in the world as we love self-lessly and offer truth that is relevant across cultures. God calls us to extend hope to the broken and hurting world.

God desires us to be influential but not influential for the sake of being influential. We are called to be influential for Jesus! This is Jesus's way of influence.

Here are a few ways that truth and love work together to bring us influence in our families, workplaces, neighborhoods, and communities.

Truth Plus Love Means God's Power Will Rest on Us

As I wrote in the last chapter, when we walk in obedience to the Word of God, our lives gain an incredible power. God's Word has the power to save, transform, change, and do what the world says in impossible.

When you read your Bible, meditate on it, and apply it to how you live your everyday life, you will sense God is with you in a greater way. There will be an unusual power in your life as you attempt to follow God wholeheartedly.

Do you read your Bible? Maybe you read your Bible, but you refuse to change a thought pattern or habit in your life to obey it.

We need to build our lives around the truth of Jesus and help others to do the same. The truth of Jesus is the power source we need to change the world.

Truth Plus Love Means Loving People Who Are Hard to Love

God loves people with a mind-boggling love. He loved the world so much that He gave everything to bring people back to Him. He wants us to love like He does.

Loving others often looks like kindness, gentleness, and respect. The closer we get to Jesus, the sweeter we should be toward other people. We shine the love of God on them.

Jesus calls us to love everyone, even our enemies, but some Christians are known for tearing everyone down in the name of truth. This should not be. We should be known for our love, and that love should lead us to self-control. We can always speak truth with love. When we share truth with gentleness, kindness, and respect, it gives us influence for the sake of the gospel and the glory of God.

What if we showed grace to the people who gossip about us? What if we offered kindness to someone who has been unkind to us? What if we showed kindness to the people we typically rush past—baristas, cashiers, customer service reps. Everyone is lovingly created in the image of God. What if we responded in kindness to someone difficult? Who can you show uncommon love to?

The Bible says, "As far as it depends on you, be at peace with all men" (Romans 12:18). Part of living in peace and love depends on us, and part depends on others. Sometimes, other people make it impossible to live at peace with them. We can only control our responses. I'm sure the apostle Paul didn't try to get together for coffee with the people who persecuted him wherever he preached the gospel. That doesn't mean he didn't try to live at peace. We should do what we can and let God worry about the rest.

Truth Plus Love Means Checking Our Motives

Don't just say you love others or pretend you care—really care for them! Really, truly, selflessly love others. We can do this by leading with our actions and asking God for our hearts to follow. When we talk about walking in truth and love, we want this to be genuine, deep down in our hearts. Pray over and over for God to do this inside of you by His Spirit.

We don't seek influence with others so we can control them for our own gain. We need to commit our motives to the Lord so our love is authentically rooted in our hearts.

We all need to look within ourselves from time to time to resubmit our motives to the Lord. It is an amazing feeling when your motives are attuned to the glory of God and to wanting what's best for others.

Truth Plus Love Means Focusing on What's Most Important to God

As Christians, we need to build our lives around what God cares about. Scripture shows us God's priorities:

- Living to worship God for the glory of God
- Serving the hurt and broken
- Prioritizing people over projects
- Telling people about the truth of Jesus
- Building up the local church
- Giving the best of ourselves to our loved ones

Truth Plus Love Means Excellence in Our Work

Our faith should affect our work. We should work as if we are working for the Lord. That's a big task and an exciting prospect! How can you start to walk in the fruit of the Spirit in what seem like the least spiritual areas of your life?

Martin Luther is often quoted as saying, "The Christian shoemaker does his duty not by putting little crosses on the shoes, but by making good shoes, because God is interested in good craftsmanship." If you are a nurse, you can show extra empathy to your patients and even pray for them in your personal prayer time. If you work at a call center, you can respond to angry customers with grace, even when you're frustrated. If you are a construction worker, you can refrain from crude jokes with the guys and instead encourage and uplift others in conversation. Part of serving God and being influential for the gospel is simply excelling at whatever we do. Excellence shows that we truly care about doing good work and serving others well.

My late grandfather-in-law loved the Scripture verse that noted the Christians serving in Caesar's household (Philippians 4:22). For him, the verse emphasized how God puts people in influential places to shine the truth of Jesus. Caesar, the Roman emperor, influenced the world, yet God put talented and respected Christians around him to influence him. Certainly, these Christians must have done their jobs with uncommon skill to have been placed in such influential positions. God puts His people in strategic places for His glory. A few weeks ago, I had the opportunity to hold a gathering of Christian leaders at Facebook headquarters. We were absolutely amazed to see and hear the stories of talented believers at Facebook and Instagram (Facebook owns both platforms) who are shining the truth and love of Jesus in significant ways to everyone in the company, including its leadership.

Truth Plus Love Means a Passion to Make a Difference

My wife's and my good friend Pamela sensed God's calling to be a missionary when she was a little girl. Pamela and I literally grew up together in our small church since before we can remember. She and her husband have become our great friends, and she exemplifies the fruit of the Spirit. She cares for others, listens to others, and relates to others in truth and love.

Before she married Nick, she served for several years as a missionary in an unreached area of the world. After they were married, they started to head out to their next assignment, but to their great disappointment, the financial support they needed didn't come in. I was heartbroken with them, but we all knew that God was sovereign, even when it comes to a dream of ministering in His name.

What's so amazing about Pam and Nick is that even while they're here in Minnesota, they have found a way to make a difference for God. They can't contain their passion to make a difference in the world, so they began to foster kids. They have uprooted their normal family patterns and sacrificed much to take in hurting kids who are stuck in the system. With open arms, they bring kids into their home, love on them, and include them as family members. It nearly brings me to tears to think how their disappointment has been swept away by these hurting kids whose lives are changing forever.

Wherever you are, find a place you can make a difference.

Truth Plus Love Means Serving Others

What if we no longer lived only to fulfill our own dreams but looked for ways to encourage, enable, and serve other people's dreams?

My friend Carson, a wonderful young pastor, says, "I fear for my generation, that we only want to do 'God things' when people are watching us, when we are on stage." It's easy to think the big things God wants to do happen on a stage at church on Sunday morning. Whether you are in ministry or not, you may feel this temptation. I know I do. But God hasn't called us to a platform (at church or on social media); He called us to serve His kingdom and to serve other people, even when no one is watching. Who in your life right now is God calling you to serve, encourage, build up, and open doors of opportunity for?

Mother Teresa, who spent her life caring for the dying in the slums of India, once said, "Do you think love has to be extraordinary? How does a lamp burn? Through the continuous input of small drops of oil. These are the small things of daily life: faithfulness, punctuality, small words of kindness, a thought for others. These are the true drops of love. Be faithful in small things, because it is in them that your strength lies."[6]

Truth Plus Love Means Engaging Culture, Not Scolding or Running from It

In the book *Stay the Course*, Pastor Choco De Jesus shares that we face the temptation to accommodate, oppose, or withdraw from culture, but he says all three responses are incorrect.[7]

Some Christians respond to secular culture by fiercely opposing it. They rail against the culture and draw battle lines in culture wars. It's hard for non-Christians to see any love or respect in that.

A second group of Christians respond to secular culture by withdrawing from it. This group might homeschool their kids out of fear. They might let their family only consume Christian media. They might overshelter themselves to the point where they become disconnected from how to be salt and light in the world. All their friends are Christians, and they have trouble thinking of anyone they could share the gospel with.

A third group of Christians are accommodating to their surrounding culture. They don't feel it matters to try to change anyone's minds, so they just go along with whatever culture thinks is best.

God hasn't called us to live out our faith in these ways. He has called us to engage culture with both truth and love. This doesn't mean we need to speak to every issue that arises, but we should thoughtfully share truth in love. The Bible says we are the salt of the earth. We are a light on a hill. We are called to shine the truth of Jesus into the pain and brokenness of our world. This may mean offering a kind word to someone who needs it, taking meals to a family whose loved one is sick, or grieving and praying with someone. We are called to show the love of Jesus to everyone we meet. We should love even those who are harsh or disagreeable. There can be tension between truth and love, and sometimes we might not get the balance right, but we need to stay engaged and be change-makers who carefully balance truth and love.

Truth Plus Love Means Sharing the Good News of the Gospel

Live in such a way that those who don't know Jesus but know you will come to know Jesus because they know you.

More and more, people in our culture are biblically illiterate and have never stepped foot inside a church building. D. L. Moody is often quoted as saying, "Out of one hundred men, one will read the Bible, and the other ninety-nine will read the

Christian." What he meant by this is that we are representatives of Jesus to the world. They may never read the Bible, but they will look at our lives to see what Jesus is all about. This sounds even truer today. We are representatives or ambassadors of Jesus. The most influential person in someone's life is usually a friend or neighbor, someone in close proximity. When we walk in both truth and love, we represent Jesus well to the people nearby.

One of the most memorable moments in my relationship with my late Grandpa Brown happened when I was a teenager. He and Grandma lived a few hours away. When we arrived for our visit, I saw a twinkle in his eyes that I hadn't seen before. He expressed a deeper passion for the gospel and his faith. He was sharing the truth of Jesus with the people in his community. It wasn't just church as usual anymore or going through the motions. He had a spiritual fire in his heart. I came to learn that he had been reading a book about evangelism by a man who would later become my friend, Mark Mittelberg.

Mark is a legend when it comes to sharing the truth of Jesus. He's an incredible example of walking in both truth and love.

Mark shares a powerful illustration in the book that changed my Grandpa's faith:

High potency Christianity + Close proximity to nonbelievers + Clearly presenting the truth of Jesus = Maximum impact for the gospel.[8]

This is one of the best models of effective influence for the gospel. We need to really walk the talk in our faith, but we also need to go to places where we can have conversations and grow in relationship with nonbelievers. Too many passionate

Christians are hiding inside churches. God wants us to get out into the world and find ways to connect with nonbelievers. Maybe connecting means starting a softball team, joining a book club, participating in a moms' group, or other similar ideas. If we do that, we're just getting started. We need to pray for and look for opportunities to share the truth of Jesus that has changed our lives. As we walk in truth plus love toward people and then clearly share the good news of Jesus with them, God will move in power through the simple gospel message. God can use you like he used Billy Graham. Trust that God works through us when we feel weak and inadequate. There is sufficient power in the simple gospel message to draw people to the truth of Jesus!

How will you use your influence as you walk in truth plus love? Will you help other people find the love, joy, peace, freedom, and hope you've found in Jesus?

The key to walking in truth and love is staying connected to Jesus by reading and meditating on God's Word. We must learn to follow Him in the little things of our everyday lives.

I hope you'll join me in praying for truth plus love and the fruit of the Spirit—love, joy, peace, patience, kindness, goodness, gentleness, faithfulness, and self-control—to be increasingly evident in our lives! Regularly, I find myself falling short of this standard and reminding my own heart how much I want to walk in truth and love. I long to grow closer to Jesus, to experience His great love, and to walk in truth plus love and the fruit of the Spirit with my family, friends, community, and world. There's no greater aim than representing Him well to the watching world.

Here we find our hope: as God helps us walk in truth plus love in our everyday lives, He will give us greater influence with the people around us, and together we can make an even greater impact on our world for Christ!

Imagine a world where

- We Christians practice uncommon kindness instead of better-than-thou judgment
- Outrage culture is replaced with Christ's heart of compassion for everyone
- We respond with unusual grace when people expected us to express outrage over our beliefs being questioned or trampled
- Truth is introduced not as condemnation but as a personal introduction to Jesus

This is the way of Jesus, and this is the way for anyone who calls Him Lord. It's the way of truth plus love, and its promise is influence. If we walk down this road, we will influence others for the sake of the gospel. Choice by choice, interaction by interaction, relationship by relationship, we can change the world. In every generation, God raises up His church, His people, to bring hope, healing, and change. And you're invited! This is your calling. This is your commission. Imagine it: in your everyday, in your every moment, God has so much more He wants to do through you. Imagine what the world could look like if you said yes—to uncompromising truth, to unrelenting love, to uncommon influence. That is how we change our world.

ACKNOWLEDGMENTS

I would like to thank—

MICHELLE AND OUR KIDS. First and foremost, I'd like to thank you for your extra grace with me in all the writing and rewriting of this book. Countless hours go into researching for and writing a book, and you've been extremely gracious with me through several books now. I love you.

LEE STROBEL. I'm not sure where I would be without your undeserved kindness in this process, not only for your extremely gracious foreword but also for being the catalyst for Zondervan's interest in me and this book. It means the world.

TOM DEAN. I'm so, so glad we met at *The Case for Christ* movie premiere and subsequently at Zondervan HQ several times. You and your team quickly felt like family and have been so kind and amazing to work with. I cherish your friendship.

STEPHANIE SMITH. You took this book to another level. I've learned so much from you and hope to keep learning from you in the future.

CASEY HELMICK. For your partnership and skill throughout this entire process. I'm so grateful to do ministry with you.

MARSHALL SEGAL. Thank you for your godly wisdom and direction in the early stages of the book.

THE ZONDERVAN TEAM. Along with Tom and Stephanie already mentioned, special thanks to David Morris, Robin Barnett, Matt Estel, and the rest of the Z team for your friendship, kindness, partnership on this book.

YOUNG INFLUENCERS. To my friends who joined me at Zondervan HQ a little over a year ago, I think so highly of all of you, and I'm excited about your books coming soon too!

ENDORSERS. To the leaders I admire so much who graciously endorsed this book and to all of the friends who helped spread the word about the book and its message, thank you so much.

JESUS. For saving my soul and changing my story. For teaching me grace. For filling my life with good things. Thank You for who You are.

NOTES

Preface

1. Francis Schaeffer, *The Mark of the Christian* (Downers Grove, IL: InterVarsity Press, 1970), 51–52.

Chapter 1: Where Has Our Influence Gone?

1. Joshua Freedman, "Dr. Daniel Goleman on the Origins of Emotional Intelligence," Six Seconds, January 20, 2005, https://www.6seconds.org/2005/01/30/goleman-emotional-intelligence/.
2. See Philippians 2:12–13; 1 Corinthians 15:10.

Chapter 2: Love

1. See 1 John 3:16; 4:7, 9–11, 19.
2. See 1 John 4:7–8; Psalm 119:64.
3. D. L. Moody, *The D. L. Moody Collection*, ed. James S. Bell (Chicago: Moody Press, 1997), 47–50.

Chapter 3: Joy

1. Sam Kim, "The Critical Role of Name-Calling in Our Witness: You Are 'Beloved,'" *The Exchange* (blog), *Christianity Today*, February 12, 2018, https://www.christianitytoday.com/edstetzer/2018/february/critical-role-of-name-calling-in-our-witness-you-are-belove.html.
2. "Giving Thanks Can Make You Happier," *Harvard Health Publishing*, https://www.health.harvard.edu/healthbeat/giving-thanks-can-make-you-happier.
3. Matt Chandler, "Revenge and Love," sermon, October 28, 2012, https://www.tvcresources.net/resource-library/sermons/revenge-and-love.
4. Choco De Jesus, sermon, Emanuel Christian Center, Spring Lake Park, MN, October 22, 2017, https://vimeo.com/239346750.
5. Corrie ten Boom, "Guideposts Classics: Corrie ten Boom on Forgiveness," *Guideposts*, reprinted July 24, 2014, originally published November 1972, https://www.guideposts.org/

better-living/positive-living/guideposts-classics-corrie-ten
-boom-on-forgiveness.

6. D. L. Moody, *Pleasure and Profit in Bible Study* (Chicago: Revell, 1895), chapter 1, https://www.gutenberg.org/files/36655/36655 -h/36655-h.ht.

7. Robert L. Peterson and Alexander Strauch, *Agape Leadership: Lessons in Spiritual Leadership from the Life of R.C. Chapman* (Littleton, CO: Lewis & Roth), 199–200, Kindle.

Chapter 4: Peace

1. Billy Graham, *Just As I Am: The Autobiography of Billy Graham* (New York: HarperCollins, 1997), 355.

2. J. I. Packer, *Knowing God* (Downers Grove, IL: InterVarsity Press, 1973), 136.

3. Eric Geiger and Kevin Peck, *Designed to Lead: The Church and Leadership Development* (Nashville: B&H, 2016), 73.

Chapter 5: Kindness and Gentleness

1. C. S. Lewis, *The Weight of Glory* (New York: HarperOne, 2001), 182.

2. See, for example, 1 Peter 2:1–3.

3. For additional study, consider: Romans 2:4; Titus 3:4; Zechariah 7:9; Proverbs 31:26; Proverbs 11:17; 1 Peter 3:8; 1 Peter 3:15.

4. A. T. Rowe, *D. L. Moody: The Soul Winner* (Anderson, IN: Gospel Trumpet, 1927), 37.

5. Dave Ferguson, Jon Ferguson, and Eric Bramlett, *The Big Idea: Aligning the Ministries of Your Church through Creative Collaboration* (Grand Rapids: Zondervan, 2007), 9.

6. J. M. Darley, and C.D. Batson, "'From Jerusalem to Jericho': A Study of Situational and Dispositional Variables in Helping Behavior" *Journal of Personality and Social Psychology* 27, no. 1 (1973): 100–108.

7. Melissa Moore (@MelissaMoore77), "Nothing strikes me as more contrary to a life of grace than a preoccupation with discovering the worst about other people," Twitter, June 11, 2014, https://twitter .com/MelissaMoore77/status/476869437975699458.

8. John C. Maxwell, *Put Your Dream to the Test: 10 Questions to Help You See It and Seize It* (Nashville: Nelson, 2011), 149.

Chapter 6: Faithfulness and Goodness

1. Guy Berger, "Will This Year's College Grads Job-Hop More Than Previous Grads?," LinkedIn (blog), April 12, 2016, https://blog.linkedin.com/2016/04/12/will-this-year_s-college-grads-job-hop-more-than-previous-grads.
2. Daniel Fusco (@danielfusco), "I want my life to be a testimony of God's faithfulness. I'll never be perfect, but my life can tell the story of a perfect, faithful God," Twitter, May 22, 2017, https://twitter.com/danielfusco/status/866837588811800577.

Chapter 7: Patience and Self-Control

1. Mark Batterson, *Whisper: How to Hear the Voice of God* (Colorado Springs: Multnomah, 2017), 152.
2. John Ortberg, *Soul Keeping: Caring for the Most Important Part of You* (Grand Rapids: Zondervan, 2014), 20.
3. See 1 Thessalonians 2:4; Deuteronomy 8:2; Psalm 26:2; Psalm 66:10; Proverbs 17:3; Isaiah 48:10.

Chapter 8: Truth

1. Graham, *Just As I Am*, 258.
2. Dan Piepenbring, "Chick-fil-A's Creepy Infiltration of New York City," *New Yorker*, April 13, 2018, https://www.newyorker.com/culture/annals-of-gastronomy/chick-fil-as-creepy-infiltration-of-new-york-city.
3. Graham, *Just As I Am*, 135–58; Will Graham, "The Tree Stump Prayer: When Billy Graham Overcame Doubt," Billy Graham Evangelistic Association, July 9, 2014, https://billygraham.org/story/the-tree-stump-prayer-where-billy-graham-overcame-doubt/.
4. Charles Spurgeon, *The Complete Works of C. H. Spurgeon*, vol. 17, *Sermons 968 to 1027* (Delmarva, 2015), ebook.
5. Rebecca Manley Pippert, *Hope Has Its Reasons* (New York: Harper, 1990).
6. Christine Caine, "Shame off You," CBN, video, http://www1.cbn.com/video/iT16v2/shame-off-you.

7. De Jesus, sermon, October 22, 2017, https://vimeo.com/239346750.

8. Billy Graham, "Things God Hates," Billy Graham Evangelistic Association, August 25, 2011, https://billygraham.org/decision-magazine/september-2011/things-god-hates/.

9. Augustine, *Confessions*, I.i.

10. Graham, *Just As I Am*, 697.

Chapter 9: Uncommon Influence

1. See Earl O. Roe, *Dream Big: The Henrietta Mears Story* (Ventura, CA: Regal, 1990), chapter 14.

2. Roe, *Dream Big*, 275.

3. Roe, *Dream Big*, 280.

4. Dr. Steward P. MacLennan, pastor of Hollywood Presbyterian from 1921–1941, endorsement for *Dream Big*.

5. Roe, *Dream Big*, 333.

6. Mother Teresa, *Daily Readings with Mother Teresa*, ed. Teresa de Bertodano (London: HarperCollins, 1994), 74.

7. Choco De Jesus, *Stay the Course: Finding Hope in a Drifting Culture* (Friendswood, TX: Baxter, 2016).

8. Mark Mittelberg and Bill Hybels, *Becoming a Contagious Christian* (Grand Rapids: Zondervan, 1996), 47.